Shakespeare & Commemoration

Shakespeare &

Series Editors:
Graham Holderness, *University of Hertfordshire*
Bryan Loughrey

Volume 5
Shakespeare & the Ethics of War
Edited by Patrick Gray

Volume 4
Shakespeare & Creative Criticism
Edited by Rob Conkie and Scott Maisano

Volume 3
Shakespeare & the Arab World
Edited by Katherine Hennessey and Margaret Litvin

Volume 2
Shakespeare & Commemoration
Edited by Clara Calvo and Ton Hoenselaars

Volume 1
Shakespeare & Stratford
Edited by Katherine Scheil

Shakespeare & Commemoration

Edited by
Clara Calvo and Ton Hoenselaars

berghahn
NEW YORK • OXFORD
www.berghahnbooks.com

First published in 2019 by
Berghahn Books
www.berghahnbooks.com

© 2019 Berghahn Books

Originally published as a special issue of
Critical Survey, volume 22, issue 2.

All rights reserved. Except for the quotation of short passages
for the purposes of criticism and review, no part of this book
may be reproduced in any form or by any means, electronic or
mechanical, including photocopying, recording, or any information
storage and retrieval system now known or to be invented,
without written permission of the publisher.

Library of Congress Cataloging-in-Publication Data

Calvo, Clara, 1961- editor. | Hoenselaars, A. J., 1956- editor.
Title: Shakespeare and commemoration / edited by Clara Calvo and Ton
  Hoenselaars.
Description: New York : Berghahn Books, 2019. | Series: Shakespeare and ;
  volume 2 | Includes bibliographical references and index.
Identifiers: LCCN 2019003820 (print) | LCCN 2019009462 (ebook) | ISBN
  9781789202489 (ebook) | ISBN 9781789202465 (hardback :alk. paper) |
  ISBN 9781789202472 (paperback :alk. paper)
Subjects: LCSH: Shakespeare, William, 1564-1616--Criticism and
  interpretation. | Memory in literature. | Recollection (Psychology) in
  literature.
Classification: LCC PR3069.M46 (ebook) | LCC PR3069.M46 S53 2019
  (print) |
  DDC 822.3/3--dc23
LC record available at https://lccn.loc.gov/2019003820

British Library Cataloguing in Publication Data
A catalogue record for this book is available from the British Library

ISBN 978-1-78920-246-5 hardback
ISBN 978-1-78920-247-2 paperback
ISBN 978-1-78920-248-9 ebook

Contents

Chapter 1   1
Introduction
Shakespeare and the Cultures of Commemoration
Ton Hoenselaars and Clara Calvo

Chapter 2   13
Acting as an Epitaph
Performing Commemoration in the Shakespearean History Play
Emily Shortslef

Chapter 3   27
From Jubilee to Gala
Remembrance and Ritual Commemoration
Robert Sawyer

Chapter 4   41
Shakespeare Remembered
Graham Holderness

Chapter 5   65
American Shakespeare Clubs and Commemoration
Katherine Scheil

Chapter 6
Shakespeare and 'Native Americans'
Forging Identities through the 1916 Shakespeare Tercentenary
Monika Smialkowska

78

Chapter 7
The Disciplines of War, Memory, and Writing
Shakespeare's Henry V *and David Jones's* In Parenthesis
Adrian Poole

93

Chapter 8
Monumental Play
Commemoration, Post-war Britain, and History Cycles
Anita M. Hagerman

107

Chapter 9
Afterword
'The Seeds of Time'
Graham Holderness

121

Index

147

Chapter 1
Introduction
Shakespeare and the Cultures of Commemoration[1]

Ton Hoenselaars and Clara Calvo

Over the past few decades, much attention has been devoted to the theme of 'memory' in the plays and poems of Shakespeare, but surprisingly little has been written about the ways in which this 'memory' cult interrelates with the 'cultures of commemoration' involving the playwright and poet.[2] 'Cultures of commemoration' – by which we mean a series of more or less conscious or active attempts to rehearse Shakespeare in the present, as well as efforts to guarantee the remembrance of Shakespearean occurrences past and present in the future – may be identified within Shakespeare's plays and poems, in his biography, as well as the joint afterlives of the man and his work. The Sonnets famously envisage the act of narration as one of vital commemoration, and like Hamlet's father who tells his son 'Remember me', so Hamlet the son wishes to be remembered in Horatio's account of him.[3] Cultures of commemoration abound in the Histories, which, as Emily Shortslef in our collection argues, have an epitaphic tradition all their own; Shortslef's contribution explores the epitaph's cultural significance and its commemorative force in the Histories, arguing that they subvert the expectations called for by the genre; from a site of memory, the epitaph turns into a site of

Notes for this section begin on page 10.

'unsettling' and as a memory cult is not unproblematic either, since it is continually being critiqued and challenged.

The play most explicitly occupied with traditions of history and memory is *Henry V*, and perhaps this concern is never more apparent than when King Henry – to use Jay Winter's phrase to distinguish conscious historical acts of commemoration from what he terms 'passive memory'[4] – projects the 'historical remembrance' of a battle yet unfought:

> This story shall the good man teach his son,
> And Crispin Crispian shall ne'er go by
> From this day to the ending of the world
> But we in it shall be rememberèd.[5]

With reference to the Agincourt speech in *Henry V*, Joep Leerssen and Ann Rigney have convincingly argued that Shakespeare not only kickstarted the cultures of commemoration around himself and his works, but that also the celebration of other writers across Europe began here as it fanned out from Shakespeare.[6] This subsequent process was largely unpredictable and could traverse many routes, but the original dynamic appears to have come from Stratford's greatest son.

In Shakespeare, explicit constructions of posthumous remembrance often seem possible only by means of an act of forgetting. Both in *Henry V* and in *Much Ado About Nothing*, the glorious account of the war dead provides us with a glimpse of its wry reality. Henry the Fifth, who before the Battle of Agincourt had democratically argued that the fight would 'gentle' the condition of his 'band of brothers', has no qualms later about reverting to a social hierarchy in death, and of commemorating by name those of high rank only.[7] A similar tendency may be discerned in the dialogue between Leonato and the Messenger in the opening scene of *Much Ado About Nothing*:

> Leonato: How many gentlemen have you lost in this action?
> Messenger: But few of any sort, and none of name.[8]

As Thomas Laqueur has argued with reference to these two instances in Shakespeare, they really show up a device, operative from ancient times until World War I, 'to efface the overwhelming majority of dead soldiers from public memory.'[9] In broader historical and cultural terms, however, the strategy also copies Benedict Anderson's observation about national identity, and the apparent tendency, when establishing a collective memory on the basis of some events, also to relegate others to oblivion.[10]

These and other complex cultures of commemoration do not only occur in the work of Shakespeare. Also the man Shakespeare and his work have become part of a ritual of commemoration across the centuries. In the case of Shakespeare, David Garrick's 'Great Shakespeare Jubilee' in Stratford (1769) started a trend and became the predecessor of the hundreds of festivals that have followed in its wake to commemorate the master, like the Royal Gala of 1830, discussed by Robert Sawyer in his contribution to this collection.[11] In his essay, Sawyer shows how the 1769 Jubilee and the 1830 Gala promoted a particular kind of social memory in relation to Shakespeare, as, together, they paved the way for a combination of tourism and theatre on which the Stratford Shakespeare industry still relies today. With the help of Connerton's analysis of how societies remember, Sawyer's contribution argues that celebrations in honour of Shakespeare soon became an 'invented tradition' in Hobsbawm's sense, showing that western cultures of commemoration, and Shakespeare's in particular, thrive on ritualistic practices. Such acts of remembrance have been performed in Britain and abroad, in times of peace, notably in 1864, but also in times of war, like the tercentenary of the playwright's death in 1916.[12] They have been celebrated on a relatively small scale – like the annual birthday celebrations in Stratford-upon-Avon, which, in their regularity, resemble the April meetings of the Deutsche Shakespeare-Gesellschaft – and on a worldwide scale, like the quatercentenary of Shakespeare's birth in 1964, whose historical proximity may well account for the fact that its grandeur still stands in no proportion to the current academic interest in the phenomenon. As an event, the quatercentenary of Shakespeare's birth has already been surpassed, in terms of ambition, scope, as well as its unprecedented global-cum-commercial dynamic, by the 450th celebration of the playwright's birth in 2014, and, more recently, by the global commemoration of the quatercentenary of his death in 2016.

But the Shakespeare industry does not focus on 23 April only to put on exhibitions, erect statues, mount plaques, or build theatre replicas. Given Shakespeare's historical association with England and that ever so difficult to define notion of Englishness, he is often a welcome guest at official commemorative gatherings that really concern the nation. This partly explains how, as Anita Hagerman demonstrates in her contribution to this essay collection, the Histories appeared as cycles at the Festival of Britain in 1951 which itself commemorated the Great Exhibition of 1851. However, as she astutely points out, the opportunistic theatre makers were, perhaps, less interested in commemorating Shakespeare or the Histories, than they were in asserting a new artistic creed on this occasion. Hagerman focuses on two English productions that presented the Histories as cycles in 1951, Barry Jackson and the Birmingham Rep's *Henry VI, Part Two* and Anthony Quayle's second tetralogy for the Shakespeare Memorial Theatre, and dissects their differences in aims and politics. Both productions were interested in presenting the Histories as cycles to advance their own agendas and, while doing so, they capitalised on nostalgia and a longing to define national identity at a time when a post-war, post-Empire, Austerity Britain was forced to redefine its role in international politics and world culture.

Considerably less complex was the appearance of 'Shakespeare' at the inauguration of the Channel Tunnel on 6 May 1994.[13] On the occasion of this historic event, the Théâtre Impérial de Compiègne – in collaboration with the Royal Shakespeare Company – appropriately staged Ambroise Thomas' opera about Shakespeare and Queen Elizabeth I, entitled *La Songe d'une nuit d'été* (Opéra-Comique, Paris, 20 April 1850). Also, it soon turned out that the production could serve more that just a single commemorative purpose, because on 22 November 2003 the film version of the Compiègne production of *Le Songe d'une nuit d'été* – following a short trip on the Eurostar train – was screened at London's Covent Garden (Lindbury Studio Theatre), to commemorate the quatercentenary of Elizabeth's death.

There are many modes of active commemoration other than those specifically grafted onto the playwright's biography like saints' or holy days in the church calendar. The production of the First Folio in 1623 was still an act of remembrance undertaken to 'out-liue', as Leonard Digges put it in the first dedicatory poem there, Shakespeare's 'Stratford Moniment.' This gesture, however, was to generate a response that emphatically meant to counter the hero worship of Shakespeare: the erection in 1896 of a statue in London for John Heminge and Henry Condell, Shakespeare's colleagues who took the initiative to publish his plays, as Graham Holderness demonstrates in his contribution to our collection. Several decades later, though, it was the First Folio itself that held centre stage at the celebration of its tercentenary in 1923.[14] It is along similar lines that we witness events like the celebration of 400 years of the Sonnets (2009), or the joint initiative of the German Shakespeare-Society and the European

Shakespeare Research Association to devote a conference to 400 years of *The Tempest* (2011).[15]

Instances of commemorating the writer, the plays, and the poems, inevitably enhance our appreciation of the functions of authorship, the transmission of the text, and dynamics of literary fame. However, on the whole the cultures of commemoration also tend to be complex in social and political terms, thus providing the scholar with an unusually rich and interdisciplinary site for Shakespearean research. Acts of commemoration, identified as historically specific manifestations of social memory and group attitudes may shed new light on academic and popular Shakespeare, on amateur and professional appropriations of Shakespeare, or serve as an occasion to express the ways in which social groups – like the American women's Shakespeare clubs during the early decades of the twentieth century, here rescued from oblivion as discussed by Katherine Scheil – seek to formulate and express their views on what binds the group, or how it should move forward. In her essay, Scheil shows that women's clubs all over the U.S. generated a commemorative culture of their own by enlisting Shakespeare to help in their civic programmes to advance education, women's suffrage, or community care, and in doing so transformed domestic practices into acts of commemoration. Even if at times their agenda aimed beyond the plays and poems, as Scheil argues, the commemorative acts conducted by these women's clubs help us to account for the pervasiveness of Shakespeare in American culture today.

Acts of Shakespearean commemoration performed in wartime – like those in World War I – may show up unexpected modes of allegiance, as Monika Smialkowska demonstrates with reference to several regional masques in the U.S. which sought to unite all Americans (marginally including Native Americans) behind Shakespeare, but wryly seem to have excluded the African Americans. Smialkowska's contribution shows some remarkable new research opportunities regarding the study of the 1916 tercentenary as she shows how the considerable attention granted to Percy MacKaye's New York masque *Caliban by the Yellow Sands* has led to a blurred representation of the real nature of the festivities in North America. After her study of three pageants in Georgia, Massachusetts, and North Dakota, the tercentenary in the U.S. seems less a top-down affair than has long been assumed. The variety and scope of the celebrations effectively challenge a view of the tercentenary as the product of the cultural hegemony of dominant social groups. Monika Smialkowska's essay reminds us that cultures of commemoration are not exclusively metropolitan in nature and often generate powerful local cults promoting civic pride and regional interests; for certain social groups, they may provide a measure of cultural legitimation.

Celebrations in wartime also have a tendency to polarize political views, and even to alienate the Bard. In fact, World War I, as Adrian Poole demonstrates, proved an occasion for some, like the poet David Jones in *In Parenthesis* (1937), to embark on what can perhaps best be described as a negative commemorative trajectory, an attempt to decentre Shakespeare. Poole examines how Jones, a survivor of the Somme, recreated his earliest memories of the Western Front in the tercentenary year partially through a memorialisation of Shakespeare. *Henry V*, for Jones the trench soldier, provided a quasi-shorthand language to encode experience in a fractured, fragmentary, intertextual modernist collage of verse and prose. *In Parenthesis*, however, as Poole shows, offers an alternative view of English literary history and of commemoration practice which, by decentring Shakespeare, critically contrasts with the aims behind Israel Gollancz's monumental *Book of Homage* (1916).[16]

Cultures of commemoration are unstable processes. They are no guarantee for any permanence in the individual's afterlife, not even Shakespeare's. In other words, some memories are not automatically performed 'until the ending of the world', as Henry the Fifth seems to believe.[17] Sonnet 55 alerts us to this as well, as it captures how, in the course of time, 'marble' and 'gilded monuments / Of princes' are bound to lose their original gloss, and will gather dirt that no-one seems inclined to remove. When sonnet 55 also alerts us to 'wasteful war [that] shall statues overturn', it effectively captures the fate of the Paul Fournier Shakespeare statue in Paris, which was erected in 1888, a week after the unveiling of the Gower Monument in Stratford-upon-Avon during what was obviously the climax of French statuemania.[18] The Gower Monument is still on display in Shakespeare's hometown and even though, to the annoyance of some, it is no longer in the place where it originally stood, nor in the configuration that the sculptor devised, its counterpart object in Paris no longer exists, except as a memory in its own right.[19] The Paris Shakespeare statue has vanished because on 11 October 1941 the Vichy government issued an act for the removal across France of most bronze statues, in view of the metal they would yield. In the course of the months and years that followed, statues were removed from public places across the country, and melted down for the war effort. And 'Shakespeare' did not survive the terror now known as 'The Death of the Statues.' The Fournier statue was removed on 13 December 1941.[20] Apart from the occasional academic interest, what continues to remind us of the statue is the stationary shop located diagonally across from the original site which, in the 1890s, derived the name 'À Shakespeare' (still legible on the shop facade) from its proximity at 109 boulevard Haussmann to the French monument for Stratford's greatest son.

Fortunately, the Vichy intervention did not signal the end of Shakespeare's career in France, and the playwright is more popular there than ever before. Also, the Paris Shakespeare statue has since been replaced by a garden and an open air theatre in the Bois de Boulogne ('Jardin Shakespeare'), and the activities during the recent commemorative years 2014 and 2016 demonstrate that Shakespeare is very much alive in France, and in the language of Molière.[21] Yet, there are some real lessons that cultures of commemoration research may learn from the complex 'Death of the Statues' episode involving the Paul Fournier statue in Paris.

The statue in Paris shows that 'Shakespeare' is a worldwide phenomenon. It inevitable alerts us to the fact that studying the cultures of commemoration involving Shakespeare, we must be prepared to cross regional, national, continental, and linguistic borders, continually reminding ourselves of the very plurality of the cultures we study. The now absent Paris statue further shows that the cultures of commemoration are really processes, and these need to be studied diachronically, with an ever careful eye for their proper historical and cultural contexts and traditions.

The case of the missing Paul Fournier statue also makes us see that as we acknowledge the historical dimension of the cultures of commemoration, we must be prepared for the fact that certain cultures and landmarks may have all but faded out of existence, may have become invisible, just as other modes of commemoration (like those currently developing in new, social media, like Facebook) are seeking to define alternative approaches to remembrance, to commemoration.

Finally, for the diehard Shakespearean, it might be worth remembering that the Fournier 'Shakespeare' was not the only statue in France to be melted down by the Vichy government. As 'Shakespeare' was taken off his pedestal and temporarily dumped in a Paris scrapyard, he found himself in the company of other artists including Hector Berlioz, Victor Hugo, Jean De la Fontaine, Jean-Jacques

Rousseau, Victorien Sardou, François Villon, Voltaire, and Émile Zola.[22] This situation brings into focus that still rarely explored avenue of comparative commemoration research.

Were not the earliest cultures of commemoration involving Shakespeare part of a larger cult sweeping through Europe and beyond, from the end of the eighteenth century onwards, and was it not already some time before Shakespeare that the German-born composer Georg Friedrich Handel was appropriated by the British and turned into a national hero, with a statue in Vauxhall Gardens erected in his own lifetime by popular subscription?[23] Garrick's historic 1769 Jubilee taking place no less than five years after the two-hundredth anniversary of the playwright's birth was really an afterthought. Yet, the Shakespeare cult was clearly emerging. As it got under way, it may well have eclipsed the fame of some writers, but it also triggered new events, like the centenary celebrations for Robert Burns in 1859.

Transversal connections are still waiting to be explored between the burgeoning Shakespeare cult of commemoration and the cult of European writers including Dante, Racine, Voltaire, Molière, Calderón, Cervantes, Goethe and Schiller, who were all appropriated by the secular cult of hero-as-poet worship in the nineteenth century, so well envisioned by Thomas Carlyle.[24] Comparative work on the unique phenomenon of Shakespeare as the third German classic alongside Johann Wolfgang Goethe and Friedrich Schiller shows what kind of fascinating results this may yield.[25] Naturally, in our open-ended field, such comparative research would soon provide an occasion for a number of interdisciplinary sorties, to include the commemorative fate of painters and composers, their work and their afterlives, in Europe but also beyond.[26]

Despite the obvious richness of this research area, it has long continued to suffer neglect, even in recent years. Shakespeareans have predictably, perhaps, tended to concentrate on the conspicuous key dates, and done occasional research around the time of these key dates, but many plaques and statues and festivals and other occasions on which Shakespeare and his work are commemorated have no immediate basis in biographical or bibliographical fact. This should enhance their interest, since the literary gods employ strange means to bring their will to be. In addition to devising new ways to celebrate the Bard, it seems valuable and even vital also to reflect on past practices and future research strategies into the dynamics of Shakespeare's memory.

This collection ends with an afterword in the form of a short story by Graham Holderness, appropriately entitled 'The Seeds of Time.' Underpinned by a cultural materialist study of the presence of Shakespeare in a series of great national festivals – the great Exhibition of 1851, the Festival of Britain in 1951, and the London Olympics of 2012 – this story uses imaginative methods to pursue a critical inquiry, combining documentary evidence and critical argument with imaginative speculation. To study Shakespeare diachronically through a time-line of national commemorations, the kind of work featured in this volume, is really analogous to travelling in time. Here H. G. Wells's Time Traveller, scientist, engineer, and devotee of progress, returns to the past in search of Shakespeare, and finds in the Great Exhibition a Shakespeare surprisingly assimilated to the priorities of mechanical engineering and industrial design. Shuttling forward to 1951, he discovers similar evidence, including a steam locomotive named William Shakespeare. Inadvertently coming across the London Olympics in 2012 (by carelessly setting his GPS navigation system to 'Stratford'), the Time Traveller encounters lines from *The Tempest* spoken by an impersonation of Isambard Kingdom Brunel. In this story historical, critical and scholarly questions are explored imaginatively in fictional form.[27]

Ton Hoenselaars is Professor of Early Modern English Literature at Utrecht University. He is the author of *Images of Englishmen and Foreigners in the Drama of Shakespeare and His Contemporaries* (Associated UP, 1992), and *Shakespeare Forever!* (Wereldbibliotheek, 2017). Other books and (co-)edited collections include *Shakespeare's Italy* (Manchester UP, 1993), *400 Years of Shakespeare in Europe* (U of Delaware P, 2003), *Shakespeare and the Language of Translation* (Arden Shakespeare, 2004; rev. 2012), *Shakespeare's History Plays* (Cambridge UP, 2004, 2006), and *Challenging Humanism* (U of Delaware P, 2005). More recently, he published the *Cambridge Companion to Shakespeare and Contemporary Dramatists* (2012) and *Multilingualism in the Drama of Shakespeare and His Contemporaries* (with Dirk Delabastita [John Benjamins, 2015]), and in 2016 was one of the editors of the *Cambridge Guide to the Worlds of Shakespeare* (2 vols.). He was the 2012 Sam Wanamaker Fellow at Shakespeare's Globe in London.

Clara Calvo is Professor of English at the University of Murcia (Spain). Her books include *Power Relations and Fool-Master Discourse in Shakespeare* (OPSL, 1991) and, with Jean Jacques Weber, *The Literature Workbook* (Routledge, 1998). With Jesús Tronch, she has edited *The Spanish Tragedy* for the Arden Early Modern Series (2013), and with Coppélia Kahn, *Celebrating Shakespeare: Commemoration and Cultural Memory* (Cambridge University Press, 2015). Between 2011 and 2018, she was the President of the Spanish and Portuguese English Renaissance Studies Association (SEDERI).

Notes

1. The research and preparation for this essay collection were funded by the 'Cultures of Commemoration' project (dir. Clara Calvo) of the Spanish Ministerio de Ciencia e Innovanción (MICINN). Project No. EDU2008-00453 (01/01/2009-31/12/2011).
2. The field is vast and notably includes Jonathan Baldo, 'Wars of Memory in *Henry V*', in *Shakespeare Quarterly* 47:2 (1996): 132-59; Garrett A. Sullivan Jr., *Memory and Forgetting in English Renaissance Drama: Shakespeare, Marlowe, Webster* (Cambridge: Cambridge University Press, 2005); as well as *Shakespeare, Memory and Performance*, ed. Peter Holland (Cambridge: Cambridge University Press, 2006).
3. *Hamlet*, 1.5.91. Unless otherwise noted, all citations of Shakespeare's plays are from *The Norton Shakespeare*, eds. Stephen Greenblatt, Walter Cohen, Suzanne Gossett, Jean E. Howard, and Katharine Eisaman Maus, and Gordon McMullan, 3rd ed. (New York: W. W. Norton, 2016).
4. Jay Winter, *Remembering War: The Great War between Memory and History in the Twentieth Century* (New Haven and London: Yale University Press, 2006), 9.
5. *Henry V*, 4.3.56-59.
6. Joep Leerssen and Ann Rigney, eds., *Commemorating Writers in Nineteenth-Century Europe: Nation-Building and Centenary Fever* (Houndmills: Palgrave Macmillan, 2014), 2.
7. *Henry V*, resp. 4.3.60-63 and 4.8.97-100.
8. *Much Ado About Nothing*, 1.1.5-6.
9. Thomas W. Lacqueur, 'Memory and Naming in the Great War', in *Commemorations: The Politics of National Identity*, ed. John R. Gillis (Princeton, NJ: Princeton University Press, 1994), 150-67 (p. 150).
10. On similar instances of historical ellipsis see Benedict Anderson, *Imagined Communities: Reflections on the Origin and Spread of Nationalism*, rev. edn. (London: Verso, 1999), 199-201.
11. On the earliest festivals, see also Péter Dávidházi, *The Romantic Cult of Shakespeare: Literary Reception in an Anthropological Perspective* (London: Macmillan, 1998); Christian Deelman, *The Great Shakespeare Jubilee* (New York: The Viking Press, 1964); Michael Dobson, *The Making of the National Poet: Shakespeare Adaptation and Authorship, 1660-1769* (Oxford: Oxford University Press, 1992); M. W. England, *Garrick's Jubilee* (Ohio: Ohio State University Press, 1964); I. R. Mann, 'The Garrick Jubilee at Stratford-Upon-Avon', *Shakespeare Quarterly* 1 (1950): 128-34, and ibid., 'The Royal Gala of 1830', *Shakespeare Quarterly* 14 (1963): 263-66;

Johanne M. Stockholm, *Garrick's Folly: The Shakespeare Jubilee of 1769 at Stratford and Drury Lane* (New York: Barnes and Noble, 1964); and Ina Schabert, 'Shakespeare', in *Europäische Errinnerungsorte 2: Das Haus Europa*, ed. Pim den Boer, Heinz Durchardt, Georg Kreis and Wolfgang Schmale (Munich: Oldenburg Verlag, 2012): 211-20; and Joep Leerssen, 'National Shakespeare', in *Cambridge Guide to the Worlds of Shakespeare*, ed. Bruce Smith, et al., 2 vols. (Cambridge: Cambridge University Press, 2016), II: 1064-70.
12. Recent studies of the 1864 tercentenary include Richard Foulkes, *The Shakespeare Tercentenary of 1864* (Bath: Society for Theatre Research (1984); ibid. '"Every Good Gift From Above" Archbishop Trench's Tercentenary Sermon', *Shakespeare Survey* 54 (2001): 80-88; and Antony Taylor 'Shakespeare and Radicalism: The Uses and Abuses of Shakespeare in Nineteenth-Century Popular Politics', *The Historical Journal* 45 (2002): 357-79. For material on the Shakespeare Tercentenary of 1916 see Clara Calvo, 'Shakespeare and Spain in 1916: Shakespearean Biography and Spanish Neutrality in the Great War', *Shakespeare and Spain* (The Shakespeare Yearbook 13), eds. J. M. González and Holger Klein (Lewiston, NY: Edwin Mellen, 2002): 58-76; ibid., 'Shakespeare and Cervantes in 1916: The Politics of Language', *Shifting the Scene: Shakespeare in European Culture*, eds. Balz Engler and Ladina Bezzola (Newark, DE: University of Delaware Press, 2004): 78-94; Thomas Cartelli, *Repositioning Shakespeare: National Formations, Postcolonial Appropriations* (London: Routledge, 1999); Balz Engler, 'Shakespeare in the Trenches', *Shakespeare Survey* 44 (1991): 105-11; Richard Foulkes, *Performing Shakespeare in the Age of Empire* (Cambridge: Cambridge University Press, 2006); Werner Habicht, 'Shakespeare Celebrations in Times of War', *Shakespeare Quarterly* 52 (2001): 441-55; Coppélia Kahn, 'Remembering Shakespeare Imperially: The 1916 Tercentenary', *Shakespeare Quarterly* 52 (2001): 456-78; and Luke McKernan, '"A Complete and Fully Satisfying Art on Its Own Account": Cinema and the Shakespeare Tercentenary of 1916', *Shakespeare* 3 (2007): 337-51.
13. See Ton Hoenselaars and Clara Calvo, 'Shakespeare Eurostar: Calais, the Continent, and the Operatic Fortunes of Ambroise Thomas', in *Shakespeare and Englishness*, eds. Willy Maley and Margaret Tudeau (London: Continuum, 2010), 143-60.
14. The annual Shakespeare lecture at The British Academy was devoted to the 'Tercentenary of the First Folio' with A. W. Pollard's *The Foundations of Shakespeare's Text* (London: Oxford University Press, 1923).
15. *William Shakespeare's Sonnets for the First Time Globally Reprinted. A Quatercentenary Anthology, 1609-2009*, eds. Manfred Pfister and Jürgen Gutsch (Dozwil TG Schweiz: Edition SIGNAthUR, 2009). For a selection of the proceedings of the conference devoted to 'Shakespeare's Shipwrecks: Theatres of Maritime Adventure', see *Shakespeare-Jahrbuch* 148 (2012).
16. For an indispensable analysis of Gollancz's *Book of Homage to Shakespeare*, see Coppélia Kahn, 'Remembering Shakespeare Imperially'. *The Book of Homage* was symbolically re-issued to commemorate the quatercentenary of Shakespeare's death (with an introduction by Gordon McMullan [Oxford: Oxford University Press, 2016]).
17. Notable examples of the quickly expanding body of literature devoted to the 'destruction of memory' include Michael Taussig, *Defacement: Public Secrecy and the Labor of the Negative* (Stanford, CA: Stanford University Press, 1999); Rudy Koshar, *From Monuments to Traces: Artifacts of German Memory, 1870-1990* (Berkeley, CA: University of California Press, 2000); and Kirrily Freeman, '"Pedestals Dedicated to Absence": The Symbolic Impact of the Wartime Destruction of

French Bronze Statuary', in *France and Its Spaces of War: Experience, Memory, Image*, ed. Patricia M. E. Lorcin and Daniel Brewer (Houndmills: Palgrave Macmillan, 2009), 163-77.
18. Michael Kimberley, *Lord Ronald Gower's Monument to Shakespeare* (Stratford-upon-Avon: The Stratford-upon-Avon Society, 1989).
19. Michael Rosenthal, 'Shakespeare's Birthplace in Stratford: Bardolatry Reconsidered', in *Writers Houses and the Making of Memory*, ed. Harald Hendrix (New York and London: Routledge, 2008), 31-44.
20. Kirrily Freeman, *Bronzes to Bullets: Vichy and the Destruction of French Public Statuary, 1941–1944* (Stanford, CA: Stanford University Press, 2009); and Elizabeth Campbell Karlsgodt, 'Recycling French Heroes: The Destruction of Bronze Statues under the Vichy Regime', *French Historical Studies* 29:1 (Winter 2006): 143-81.
21. For the history of the 'Jardin Shakespeare', see *Shakespeare Companies and Festivals: An International Guide*, ed. Ron Engle, Felicia Hardison Londré, and Daniel J. Water Meier (Westport, CT: Greenwood Press, 1995), 414-17. For further details, see Ton Hoenselaars, 'The Paul Fournier Shakespeare Statue in the City of Paris, 1888-1941: Reflections on Commemoration, Cosmopolitanism, and Urban Development during the Third Republic', *Shakespeare-Jahrbuch* 147 (2011), 105-23. On recent commemorative events in France, see 'Shakespeare 450: A Jubilee in Paris' at https://journals.openedition.org/shakespeare/2910.
22. For further examples, consult the Paris statues catalogue in Jacques Lanfranchi, *Les Statues des grands hommes à Paris* (Paris: L'Harmattan, 2004), 205-64. See also Jean Cocteau, *La Mort des statues*. Photographies de Pierre Jahan. Préface de Pascal Ory (Paris: Les Éditions de l'Amateur, 2008).
23. See William Weber, 'The 1784 Handel Commemoration as Political Ritual', *The Journal of British Studies* 28 (1989): 43-69; and Suzanne Aspden, '"Fam'd Handel Breathing, tho' Transformed to Stone": The Composer as Monument', *Journal of the American Musicological Society*, 55 (2002): 39-90.
24. For a general discussion, see Ronald Quinault, 'The Cult of the Centenary, c. 1784-1914', *Historical Research* 71:176 (1998): 303-23. For individual authors, see a.o. Albert Schinz, 'The Racine Tercentenary in France', *The French Review* 13 (1940): 199-210; and Stephen Bird, *Reinventing Voltaire: The Politics of Commemoration in Nineteenth-Century France* (Oxford: Voltaire Foundation, 2000). For a broader European perspective, see *Europa: Notre Histoire*, ed. Étienne François and Thomas Serrier (Paris: Les Arènes, 2017).
25. See *Shakespeare–Goethe–Schiller*, theme issue of *Shakespeare-Jahrbuch* 141 (2005).
26. Pointing in the right direction are Joep Leerssen and Ann Rigney in *Commemorating Writers in Nineteenth-Century Europe*, as well as Paul Westover and Ann Wierda Rowland (eds.), *Transatlantic Literature and Author Love in the Nineteenth Century* (Houndmills: Palgrave Macmillan, 2016). In this connection, one should not ignore 'Shakespeare Feiern' [= Celebrating Shakespeare], theme issue of *Shakespeare-Jahrbuch* 151 (2015).
27. For a critical account of the same material, see Graham Holderness, 'Remembrance of Things Past: Shakespeare 1851, 1951, 2012', in *Celebrating Shakespeare: Commemoration and Cultural Memory*, ed. Clara Calvo and Coppélia Kahn (Cambridge: Cambridge University Press, 2015), 78-100.

Chapter 2
Acting as an Epitaph
Performing Commemoration in the Shakespearean History Play

Emily Shortslef

The epitaph is arguably the paradigmatic form of textual commemoration: not only is it a genre devoted exclusively to remembering the dead, but its (real or imagined) physical proximity to the deceased – the word derives from the Greek *epi-taphos*, 'on the tomb' – also lends the epitaph an aura that suggests an intimacy, even continuity, with the person it memorialises. If this is most readily apparent in those epitaphs that speak in the first person, inviting their readers to see in the 'I' of the verse both the voice of the dead and the textual inscription itself, a similar position of speaking for or on behalf of, rather than simply *about* the deceased, is assumed by all epitaphs. The epitaph posits itself as a privileged mediator between the dead and the living at the very site where the two meet, enabling a fantasy of direct or almost-direct address.[1] The idea of a tombstone inscription suggests a narrowing of the distance inherent to the act of remembrance; it allows one to imagine commemoration in terms of the dead speaking for themselves, or the living for them, but closely and personally, with knowledge both intimate and authoritative. Hence the persistence of 'epitaph' or 'epitaphic' as descriptors of commemorative texts that seem uncannily to represent the dead as both absent and present.

Notes for this section begin on page 24.

If these are recognizably modern connotations of 'epitaph', they are also discernibly emergent in many early modern usages of the word. In his *Quoting Death*, Scott Newstok suggests that the post-Reformation shift to textual memorial practices serves as a catalyst for what he argues is an unprecedented preoccupation with epitaphs in sixteenth-century England, a phenomenon evidenced by a wealth of references to and quotations of epitaphs within other discourses of the period. Newstok proposes that when early modern writers 're-*cited* and re-*sited* (as in re-*situated*) these texts within new contexts', their work performs what he calls a 'mutual test case for both the simple and complex genres', in which the incorporating genre negotiates some of its own problems through its encounter with and transformation of similar tensions within the epitaphic genre.[2] These tensions arise from the epitaph's presumed capacity uniquely to represent the dead and maintain their connection to the living.

It is this perceived ability of the epitaph to speak for the dead with particular force and truth that Shakespeare draws upon and undermines when he embeds or invokes epitaphs in his work: Hamlet declares that it 'were better [to] have a bad epitaph' than be castigated in the players' performances, the *Sonnets* disavow the commemorative potential of monuments and their inscriptions alike, the epitaphs composed for Hero and Marina's tombs in *Much Ado About Nothing* and *Pericles* tell lies.[3] These and other examples of Shakespearean epitaphs lead Newstok to conclude that Shakespeare recognizes the fundamentally 'staged' quality of the supposedly sincere epitaphic genre.[4] Arguing that Shakespeare's epitaphs demonstrate a certain scepticism about the potential of inscriptions to preserve the memory of the dead, Anita Gilman Sherman likewise suggests that the playwright's use of epitaphs exposes their generic pretensions.[5]

This essay focuses on a type of epitaphic incorporation in Shakespearean drama different from that considered by Newstok and Gilman, expanding the scope of 'epitaph' to include what would more accurately be described as the staging of embodied epitaphic performances than the staged reading of embedded textual epitaphs. In the examples I consider, characters literalize a common early modern epitaphic trope of the living acting as epitaphs for the dead. Recognizing these instances as epitaphs broadens the ways in which we might think about Shakespeare's treatment of the genre as well as its potential for ideological work within other literary texts and elsewhere. I argue that in Shakespeare's English history plays, embodied epitaphs, far from demonstrating the failure or insincerity of the epitaph as a memorial, function as a vehicle for a critique that assumes the genre's *success* at eliciting certain commemorative performances from its audience. The objects of this critique are these performances of memory and the relation to the past which they posit, a relation that the English history play, as well as the epitaph, is arguably complicit in reproducing.

In early modern England, epitaphs work to produce and preserve continuity between the dead and the living, the past and the present, encouraging the living to prove their remembrance of the dead by imitating their actions. Likewise, the figurative language of the plays' oratory represents the past as pushing on the present, invoking this presumed continuity to make demands of the living (in this case, the waging of war). But epitaphs in the history plays query the logic of those arguments that suggest the present should imitate the past, or that remembrance constitutes the performance of actions which maintain or create continuity between the two. They are one strategy through which the history plays, as many critics have argued, work to challenge the official narratives of the nationalist commemorative projects of which they otherwise may seem to be a part.[6] Putting this critique in the mouth of an epitaph – a text more conventionally representative of precisely this kind of argumentation – is typical of Shakespeare's ironic treatment of the genre. But the rhetorical force of the epitaph in early modern England makes it a particularly compelling counter to the logic against which it is deployed in the history plays, for while these epitaphs expose the ideological basis of the trope of the speaking dead and the ever-present past, they are also an instance of the very problem they point out. They speak for or on behalf of the dead, bringing them (uncomfortably) close, making an affectively moving, memorable, and immediate critique that is also a case for considering the past in terms of rupture, distance, and discontinuity.

As evidence of the increasing significance of epitaphs in early modern England, Newstok charts the development of the parameters of the term, from referring first to an actual tombstone inscription, then including a literary text that only imagines its location as the tomb, until eventually the reference to an 'epitaph' can function as a rhetorical gesture without any textual referent.[7] Often this is a gesture of judgement, where a hypothetical 'epitaph' signifies a summative evaluation of a person's life, to lasting honour or infamy. (Attempts at defining the genre identify this characteristic as being at the heart of the epitaph: the poetic theorist George Puttenham writes in *The Arte of English Poesie* [1589] that 'the poem called epitaph used for memorial of the dead' is 'applied to the report of the dead person's estate and degree, or of his other good or bad parts, to his commendation or reproach, and is an inscription such as a man may commodiously write or engrave upon a tomb in few verses, pithy, quick, and sententious, for the passerby to peruse and judge upon').[8] In the period, evaluative judgements of all sorts are composed or imagined as 'epitaphs.'[9] There is, then, something quite fitting about Shakespeare using the epitaph as a strategy for critique.

I would suggest that the rhetorical potency of 'epitaph' derives from the genre's association with the burial site and the body, as if it is the last word, the remainder, of the dead. What Shakespeare draws upon is the epitaph's ability to command, seemingly from beyond the grave, some type of commemorative performance from the living. From the pleas of ancient Greek roadside epitaphs that travellers would carry news of the death to neighbouring towns, to the medieval requests for prayer for the departed souls, epitaphs often urge their readers to *do* something in particular as a sign that they are serious about honouring and preserving a connection to the dead. Early modern epitaphs frequently articulate remembrance in overtly didactic terms, exhorting readers to prove their remembrance by imitating the virtuous lives of the now-deceased.[10] The speaker of Ben Jonson's epitaph for Sir Charles Cavendish, for example, instructs,

> Sonnes, seeke not me amonge these polish'd stones [...]
> I made my lyfe my monument, & yours:
> to which there's no materiall that endures;
> nor yet inscription like it. Write but that;
> And teach your nephewes it to aemulate.[11]

The reader is to incorporate the dead so thoroughly into his life that he becomes a living and walking epitaph, replacing the text. The implicit rationale for the reader to remember in this way is made explicit in another common epitaphic formula:

> As you are now, so once was I
> As I am now, so shall you be
> Therefore prepare to follow me.[12]

Epitaphs like these posit a relation of past and future likeness between the dead and the living, a likeness that motivates the present action which the inscription demands. In the process, the dead as well as the living are reduced to epitaphs – the materialization of the disembodied, demanding voice of the dead on the one hand, and, on the other, the responses of the living who attempt to re-member the dead and, by imitating them, become more like them. If these are fantasies, they are no less affectively and effectively powerful for being so: there is nothing quite like invoking the dead to inspire the living to action.

In the history plays, Shakespeare represents bodies – living and dead, dismembered appendages and excreted fluids alike – becoming epitaphs. Richard II tells Aumerle that he envisions their tears eroding the soil, creating their graves and an accompanying epitaph, '"There lies / Two kinsmen digged their graves with weeping eyes"' (*Richard II* 3.3.167–8), King Edward threatens to cut off Warwick's head and 'Write in the dust this sentence with thy blood: / "Wind-changing Warwick now can change no more"' (*3 Henry VI* 5.1.56–7), and the ghosts of those for whose deaths he is responsible appear to Richard III as an epitaphic memento mori of sorts, a series of commands to 'think on me' (*Richard III* 5.5.88). Shakespeare's contemporary Thomas Nashe suggests that the enactment of the history play is itself an embodied epitaphic performance, staged for the benefit of the living, to the imagined approval of the dead. Of *1 Henry VI*, Nashe proclaims:

> How would it have joyed brave Talbot, the terror of the French, to think that after he had lain two hundred years in his tomb, he should triumph again on the stage, and have his bones new embalmed with the tears of ten thousand spectators at least (at seuerall times), who in the tragedian that represents his person, imagine they behold him fresh bleeding![13]

In Nashe's rendering, the history play offers a commemoration of the English past so immediate and lifelike that the dead can be encountered by the living in the present as if they were actually alive and present (if only to be killed off again). In referring to the 'new embalming' of the military hero, Nashe ascribes a particular potency to the spectators' imagined tears: Talbot is resurrected to show contemporary audiences how far they have fallen from the model of the past, and to spur them to reform. Those tears are proof of their desire to be worthy of the past, to become like it; Talbot can rest in peace because he has triumphed over the sixteenth-century English as well as the fifteenth-century French. Nashe is, after all, defending the theatre, and his point is the efficacy of the vivid, immediate theatrical performance to produce other performances outside its walls: 'Our forefathers' valiant acts, that have lain long buried in rusty brass and worm-eaten books, are revived, and they themselves raised from the grave of oblivion, and brought to plead their aged honours in open presence: than which, what can be a sharper reproof to these degenerate effeminate days of ours?' he asks.[14] Encountering the past in this way, the present is made to remember, and encouraged to imitate, its deeds.

Within the history plays themselves, characters make the case for waging war using similar terms, insisting on the necessity of either maintaining an existing or activating a latent relation of similarity and continuity to the glorious military achievements of the past. Just as Nashe argues that the performance of Talbot on the English stage can serve as a corrective example, characters in the plays bring up figures from the past to shame or inspire their own audiences. In *Henry V*, for instance, the king's advisors remind him of his predecessors Edward III and Edward the Black Prince, urging him to

> Awake remembrance of these valiant dead
> And with your puissant arm renew their feats,

and

> Stand for your own; unwind your bloody flag;
> Look back into your mighty ancestors,
> Go, my dread lord, to your great-grandsire's tomb,
> From whom you claim; invoke his warlike spirit.[15]

Canterbury suggests that if the king performs the same warlike actions as his ancestors, it is as if he revives them: 'You are their heir; you sit upon their throne; / The blood and courage that renowned them / Runs in your veins', he insists.[16] King Henry himself also uses organic or bodily metaphors to suggest an unbroken line stretching from the past to the present, figuring the mandate to participate within a larger collective identity in terms of the blood relation between fathers and sons. Before Harfleur, he reminds his soldiers of the service their fathers did for England, and demands that the men prove their honourable remembrance of those fathers by imitating their actions in battle. He phrases this as a test of their parentage: 'Dishonour not your mothers; now attest / That those whom you call'd fathers did beget you', he commands, addressing the gentlemen as 'you noblest English, / Whose blood is fet from fathers of war-proof,

/ Fathers that like so many Alexanders / Have in these parts from morn till even fought', and asking the yeomen 'whose limbs were made in England' to 'show us here / The mettle of your pasture; let us swear / That you are worth your breeding'.[17] At the same time, however, the king's St Crispin's Day speech promises a transcendence of blood through its mutual shedding – 'For he today that sheds his blood with me / Shall be my brother; be he ne'er so vile, / This day shall gentle his condition', an unlikely pledge accompanied by the evocation of an imaginary future in which those men might become memorable examples themselves.[18] The dead and the not-yet-living thus become causes and rationales for war, urging men to military action and praising them for it. A lack of action, conversely, is a failure of memory, a failure of blood and limbs to be put to their proper uses.

But while early modern commemorative texts and practices that go by the name 'epitaph' conventionally assert or argue for the continuity between past and present, encouraging this type of living memorial by asking the reader to embody or imitate the virtues and actions of the dead, the epitaphs in Shakespeare's history plays, as elsewhere in his work, subvert the expectations of their genre and function as sites that unsettle. Rather than working to *correct* any difference and distance between the imagined past and the present, as Nashe argues that staged representations of long-dead heroes might, they disrupt the seamlessness of the rhetoric of continuity and similitude that the plays' oratory frequently uses as a call to war.

These epitaphs, to which I will now turn, are not tombstone inscriptions, but extemporaneous epitaphs orally recited on the battlefield over unburied bodies. Characters serve as epitaphs for other characters slain in war, performing the traditional epitaphic functions of identifying the corpse (often with deictic 'here lies' gestures), speaking for the dead, and urging action on behalf of the fallen. Here the trope of becoming an epitaph is literalized, exposing the death that lurks beneath the veneer of the notion of the living, performed memorial, and mirroring back to the figurative language of the oratory its contorted logic. And yet, as statements of mourning made over the dead – one can imagine the actor holding another in his arms, or crouched over his body – these epitaphs meet the oratory's stirring invocation of the obligations of remembrance on its own affective ground: the dead seem so immediate and so visible that what they say appears especially urgent, especially moving, and this is part of the strength of the critique they articulate.

Identifying a corpse may be the most banal epitaphic convention, but it quickly becomes tragic when the identity of the dead is unexpected, as it is in a scene from *3 Henry VI* that parodies, to wrenching effect, the idea that one's actions in war would demonstrate the resemblance between sons and fathers. A soldier, entering with a dead body in his arms, lifts up the man's helmet to identify him. 'Who's this?' he asks, then recoils: 'O God! It is my father's face / Whom in this conflict I, unwares, have killed'.[19] Weeping, he begs, 'pardon, father, for I knew not thee'.[20] Almost immediately he is followed by another soldier carrying a body. Removing the helmet from the corpse, the second soldier cries, 'But let me see: is this our foeman's face? / Ah, no, no, no – it is mine only son!'.[21] Although the oratory of the history plays figures a soldier's belonging to a collective identity in terms of imitating his father's military performance, war – supposedly the occasion for sons to prove both their resemblance to their fathers and their fitness to serve as examples for their own sons – is revealed here to be the source of tragic discontinuities that prevent fathers and sons from even recognizing each other until it is too late for identification to come in any form but that of an epitaph. 'O bloody times', King Henry VI laments, witnessing the 'piteous spectacle'.[22]

Once they have, to their horror, identified the dead, the men express over the bodies a series of statements that amount to the traditional epitaphic formula of becoming a living memorial to the deceased. The second soldier, holding his son, promises that 'These arms of mine shall be thy winding sheet; / My heart, sweet boy, shall be thy sepulchre, / For from my heart thine image ne'er shall go. / My sighing breast shall be thy funeral bell' (2.5.114–17), the sense of grief heightened by the knowledge that the same body that is now figuratively to serve as his son's memorial was first literally the instrument of his death. Knowing that they, as epitaphs, must pass on the news of the deaths, the soldiers imagine the outrage they will incur upon revealing how their relatives died. 'How will my mother for a father's death / Take on with me, and ne'er be satisfied!' the first soldier wonders. 'How will my wife for slaughter of my son / Shed seas of tears, and ne'er be satisfied!' the second soldier adds. 'How will the country for these woeful chances / Misthink the King, and not be satisfied!' Henry chimes in, reiterating the dreadfulness of the war while also worrying about what these tragedies might mean for his own legacy.[23] Serving as epitaphs for their own family members results in the soldiers' undoing of the conventional request of the oratorical example for its audience to commemorate the dead by imitating their actions in battle. Their remembrance instead takes the form of an explicit *refusal* to participate in the war any longer or put their arms to use as weapons: 'I'll bear thee hence, and let them fight that will – / For I have murdered where I should not kill', the second soldier says as he carries away his son's body.[24] The first soldier also exits with his father's corpse and a promise to 'bear thee hence where I may weep my fill'.[25]

Traditionally the epitaph and the oratorical use of the example each attempt to mobilize the living to action on behalf of the dead. When the epitaphs of the history plays speak as the dead, they expose how patently self-serving (if rhetorically forceful) this fiction is, for the dead tend to say exactly what the living would like them to say. While this is not unique to the history plays' epitaphs, the undisguised frankness of their ventriloquism makes their motivation particularly visible. In *1 Henry VI*, for instance, Talbot imagines himself speaking in Salisbury's voice a vengeful epitaph that urges a renewed onslaught against the French and positions the dead nobleman as an example for the rest of the English soldiers to imitate. Carrying Salisbury's body, Talbot cries, 'He beckons with his hand, and smiles on me, / As who should say, "When I am dead and gone, / Remember to avenge me on the French"'.[26] The obvious liberty which Talbot takes in putting words in Salisbury's mouth reveals both the ease and the awkwardness with which the speechless dead can be made to say anything that suits the purposes of the living.

In terms of the plot, Salisbury's death and the epitaph that Talbot speaks for him bear no relation to the continued assault on the French but only add a commemorative motive to what Talbot was going to have his men do anyway. While the influence such a motive can have may seem minimal, Talbot's complaint as the English retreat is a reminder of the efficacy of invoking or ventriloquizing the dead to shame an audience into action. As his men are beaten back by the French, Talbot accuses them of having 'all consented unto Salisbury's death, / For none would strike a stroke in his revenge'.[27] Like Henry V's suggestion to his soldiers that failing to imitate the warlike actions of their fathers dishonours the reputations of their mothers, Talbot implies that retreat is both an insult to the memory of Salisbury and an indication that they never cared for him in the first place. The absurdity of such an argument is highlighted by the obviously false causal connection Talbot posits between Salisbury's death and the soldiers' inability to avenge it, but the sense of shame such a statement attempts to produce is nevertheless quite palpable.

Although he fails to make the epitaph he invents for Salisbury into an example for his men to follow, Talbot's vow to 'be a Salisbury' to the French culminates eventually in his own death at the hands of the French, a fate that reverberates in Burgundy's eerily epitaphic promise to the still-living 'warlike and martial Talbot' to 'enshrine thee in his heart, and there erect / Thy noble deeds as valour's monuments'.[28] In the history plays the living memorial the example urges is always bordering on the epitaphic; in the desire of the living to be like the dead, the living often end up resembling the dead more than they would like. Westmorland's pseudo-epitaphic comment in *Henry V* regarding the English hearts that 'lie pavilioned in the fields of France', although it ostensibly intends only to suggest the willingness of the king's men to fight on his behalf, prefigures the bodies that will actually lie strewn across French fields.[29]

Likewise, in the same play King Henry's oratorical singling out of blood and limbs to represent the continuity of lineage and strength has a literal counterpart in the things that are actually lost on the battlefield. While he imagines the actions of limbs heroically proving the relation between sons and their fathers, these parts, when given actual voices, speak of their sundering from the body and serve as reminders of the cost of war. The night before the Battle of Agincourt, King Henry's soldiers, not recognizing the disguised king in their midst, talk unguardedly about the death that very likely awaits them. Williams warns that,

> If the cause be not good, the King himself hath a heavy reckoning to make, when all those legs and arms and heads chopped off in a battle shall join together at the latter day, and cry all, 'We died at such a place' – some swearing, some crying for a surgeon, some upon their wives left poor behind them, some upon the debts they owe, some upon their children rawly left.[30]

While the history plays' oratory frequently encourages its audience to think of their own actions as establishing examples for the future, just as they look to the past for patterns to emulate, this speech offers a disconcerting view of what epitaphs might tell the future about those actions. War, in Williams's account, is not a glorious opportunity for sons to prove their continuity with their fathers or establish their place within a collective group, but rather a profoundly *disrupt-*

ing event that takes men away from their responsibilities, leaves their families destitute, and even endangers their souls.

When Henry V later prays that God will take from his soldiers 'the sense of reck'ning' he means most directly the ability to count their foes, who outnumber them, but he may be referring as well to the 'heavy reckoning' to which Williams alludes when he says 'if these men do not die well, it will be a black matter for the King that led them to it'.[31] Williams's reference to the king before God on Judgement Day is a dark parody of Henry's St Crispin's Day longing for his name to be remembered until the ending of the world; it also resonates with the king's earlier declaration, on the eve of war, that

> Either our history shall with full mouth
> Speak freely of our acts, or else our grave,
> Like Turkish mute, shall have a tongueless mouth,
> Not worshipped with a waxen epitaph.[32]

Most strikingly, however, Williams's warning suggests the capacity of the bodies of the oppressed to serve as epitaphs, for the chilling evocation of the scattered pieces of resurrected corpses joining together envisions the dismembered limbs as all these little epitaphs, telling where and how they died, witnesses to the injustices of history. Each of these forensic epitaphs, each with its own voice, might give damning testimony against the king. Aside from accusing him of leading soldiers into war foolishly and demanding justice for the losses suffered under his command, the epitaphs, which literalize the figure of the dead that still speak and live, might reveal other truths as well: the dead might not endorse the actions of the living, might argue for rupture rather than resemblance between the past and the present, might remember things some would prefer them to forget. Little wonder, then, that in the king's fantasy, if history cannot speak with a mouth full of praise, it should not speak at all, even – or especially – with an epitaph.

King Henry envisions oblivion as an epitaph-less grave, positing the epitaph as the thing on which memory hinges, and indeed, the 'waxen epitaph' speech, which closes on an image of a mutilated mouth, hints at the various kinds of forgetting that are inherent to any culture's production of collective memory. Far from demonstrating Shakespeare's indifference to or scepticism about the capability of epitaphs to be agents of commemoration, this remark, juxtaposed with the function of epitaphs in the history plays, suggests his awareness of the potency of the 'epitaph', although less as a genre than as representative of a certain relation to the past. For while the comparison of an epitaph to a tongue forcibly removed from the mouth of a slave acknowledges the threat it poses – an epitaph can be an undesired memorial, a 'tongue' that speaks damning things – what epitaphs in the history plays remember is primarily the ruptures that the figurative language of the oratory masks. They work against some of the commemorative imperatives posed within the history play; in particular, they challenge the notion that remembering the past necessitates proving a likeness or continuity between it and the present. If this is the relation to the past that the 'epitaphic' more conventionally proposes, the English history plays exploit the epitaph's cultural significance to critique this relation, drawing on the affective force of the epitaphic to imagine the dead saying something else, for Shakespeare's epitaphs here demonstrate the *fantasy* of the epitaphic discourse: the dead are gone; it is only the effects of the past that linger, and if the commemorative action proposed is remembering the past by imitating its wars, perhaps the present should dare to let it go.

Emily Shortslef is Assistant Professor of English at the University of Kentucky. Her work has appeared in the *Journal for Early Modern Cultural Studies* and *Exemplaria*, and is forthcoming in *ELH*. She is currently completing a book manuscript entitled *Shakespeare and the Drama of Complaint*, which explores the intersections between Shakespearean drama, moral philosophy, and early modern discourses of complaint.

Notes

1. Paul de Man makes this point in 'Autobiography as De-facement', *Comparative Literature* 94 (1979): 919–30, one of the most influential theorisations of epitaphic discourse.
2. Scott Newstok, *Quoting Death in Early Modern England: The Poetics of Epitaphs Beyond the Tomb* (Basingstoke: Palgrave Macmillan, 2009), 4, 25. Emphasis in original.
3. *Hamlet*, 2.2.505. Unless otherwise noted, all citations of Shakespeare's plays are from *The Norton Shakespeare*, ed. Stephen Greenblatt, Walter Cohen, Jean E. Howard, and Katharine Eisaman Maus, 2nd edn. (New York and London: W.W. Norton, 2008).
4. Newstok, *Quoting Death*, 136–68.
5. Anita Gilman Sherman, *Skepticism and Memory in Shakespeare and Donne* (New York: Palgrave Macmillan, 2007), 168–80.

6. On the importance of Shakespeare's English history plays to the (re)production of a national past see Phyllis Rackin, *Stages of History: Shakespeare's English Chronicles* (Ithaca, NY: Cornell University Press, 1990); Richard Helgerson, *Forms of Nationhood: The Elizabethan Writing of England* (Chicago: University of Chicago Press, 1992); and Jean E. Howard and Phyllis Rackin, *Engendering a Nation: A Feminist Account of Shakespeare's English Histories* (London and New York: Routledge, 1997). Critics who have recently suggested reading the English history plays through the lens of cultural memory include Jonathan Baldo, '"Into a thousand parts": Representing the Nation in *Henry V*', *English Literary Renaissance* 38 (2008): 55-83, and id. *Memory in Shakespeare's Histories: Stages of Forgetting in Early Modern England* (London and New York: Routledge, 2012); Donald Hedrick, 'Advantage, Affect, History, *Henry V*', *PMLA* 118 (2003): 470-87; and Christopher Ivic, 'Reassuring Fratricide in *1 Henry IV*', in *Forgetting in Early Modern English Literature and Culture*, ed. Christopher Ivic and Grant Williams (London and New York: Routledge, 2004), 99-109. These studies locate the various battles and conflicts staged by the English history plays within a larger set of clashes over memory, specifically the selection of events and people to be commemorated.
7. Newstok, *Quoting Death*, 14-15.
8. George Puttenham, '*The Art of English Poesy' by George Puttenham: A Critical Edition*, ed. Frank Whigham and Wayne A. Rebhorn (Ithaca, NY: Cornell University Press, 2007), 144.
9. One common instance of this tendency can be found in early modern sermons, which frequently summarize a notorious individual's life with the satirical phrase 'and his epitaph was …' even when it is evident that no such tombstone inscription actually exists. See, for example, Thomas Adams, *The devil's banket described in four sermons* (London: Printed by Thomas Snodham for Ralph Mab, 1614), Early English Books Online. Adams announces that 'It was Epitaph'd on Pope Alexanders Tombe, *Iacet hîc ⁊ scelus ⁊ vitium*. Here lies wickednesse it selfe: it could not bee so buried vp'. Shakespeare's characters also refer to the epitaph as a form of judgement: in *Cymbeline*, Belarius describes 'the toil o' th' war' as 'a pain that only seems to seek out danger / I'th' name of fame and honour, which dies i'th' search / And hath as oft a sland'rous epitaph / As record of fair act', complaining that despite all his attempts at honour through obedience to a monarch and military duty in his service, history will still judge him (incorrectly) with reproach (3.3.49-53). Likewise, Prince Hal seems to recognize the potential of an epitaph to be an unflattering historical record when, standing over the body of his fallen enemy, he tells Hotspur, 'Adieu, and take thy praise with thee to heaven. / Thy ignominy sleep with thee in the grave, / But not remembered in thy epitaph' (*1 Henry IV*, 5.4.99-101).
10. Joshua Scodel argues that the primary purpose of early modern epitaphs is to maintain the place of the dead in the social order and preserve continuity with the past. See Joshua Scodel, *The English Poetic Epitaph: Commemoration and Conflict from Jonson to Wordsworth* (Ithaca, NY: Cornell University Press, 1991).
11. Ben Jonson, 'Sir Charles Cavendish To His Posteritie', in *Ben Jonson*, ed. C. H. Herford, Percy Simpson, and Evelyn Simpson, 11 vols. (Oxford: Clarendon Press, 1925-52), 8: 387-88.
12. Newstok finds this to be the most common epitaphic formula in early modern England (*Quoting Death*, 30).
13. *Pierce Penniless his Supplication to the Devil* (1592), *Thomas Nashe: The Unfortunate Traveller and Other Works*, ed. J.B. Steane (London: Penguin, 1972), 113.

14. *Pierce Penniless his Supplication to the Devil*, 113.
15. Respectively *Henry V*, 1.2.115–16 and 1.2.100–104.
16. *Henry V*, 1.2.117–19.
17. Respectively *Henry V*, 3.1.22–23, 3.1.19–20, and 3.1.26–28.
18. *Henry V*, 4.3.61–63.
19. *Henry VI*, 2.5.61–62.
20. *3 Henry VI*, 2.5.70.
21. *3 Henry VI*, 2.5.82–83.
22. *3 Henry VI*, 2.5.73.
23. *3 Henry VI*, 2.5.103–108.
24. *3 Henry VI*, 2.5.121–22.
25. *3 Henry VI*, 2.5.113.
26. *1 Henry VI*, 1.6.70–72.
27. *1 Henry VI*, 1.7.34–35.
28. Respectively *1 Henry VI*, 1.6.84 and 3.6.4–6.
29. *Henry V*, 1.2.129.
30. *Henry V*, 4.1.128–34,
31. *Henry V*, 4.1.273, 136–37.
32. *Henry V*, 1.2.230–33.

Chapter 3
From Jubilee to Gala
Remembrance and Ritual Commemoration

Robert Sawyer

> '*I accept Shakespeare's memory.*' (Borges, 'Shakespeare's Memory')

In Jorge Luis Borges' short story 'Shakespeare's Memory', we come upon Professor Sörgel, the narrator, as he attends a Shakespeare conference in London. During a drinking session at a local pub, a fellow conference attendee offers him Shakespeare's recollections – 'from his youngest boyhood days to early April, 1616'.[1] Once he accepts the gift, however, he is warned that the memory will come somewhat gradually, for it 'must be "discovered", as it will emerge in dreams or when [he is] awake', or, equally important, as he turns 'the pages of a book or turn[s] a corner'.[2] As Shakespeare's memory starts to surface, the narrator expresses his surprise that the memories he has acquired are not 'primarily visual' but pour forth in Elizabethan speech and simple melodies he had never heard before, 'a good deal more auditory than visual'.[3] After a month, 'the dead man's memory had come to animate [him so] fully' that he begins to lose his own recollections in the deluge of Shakespeare's: 'At first the waters of the two memories did not mix; in time, the great torrent of Shakespeare threatened to flood [his] own modest stream – and very nearly [does] so'.[4] Eventually, he passes the memory on to a willing recipient, as his own returns, although he is still on occasion, 'unsettled by small, fleeting memories' that are 'perhaps authentic'.[5]

Notes for this section begin on page 37.

Borges' short story evokes a number of issues germane to Shakespearean commemoration: the desire for authentic recollection, the auditory evocation of the past, the iconic images that may symbolize former events, and the need to institutionalize Shakespearean memories both personally and publicly. In the essay that follows, I hope to show how two Stratfordian celebrations – Garrick's Jubilee in 1769 and the Royal Gala of 1830 – further a type of social memory dedicated to Shakespeare and his works, a latter-day attempt to 'keepe the memory of so worthy a Friend, & Fellow aliue, as was our SHAKESPEARE', as John Heminge and Henry Condell put it.

In 1769, David Garrick staged the first, and perhaps the best-known, of the many Stratford-based tributes to Shakespeare. Variously called the Shakespeare Jubilee on the one hand, or Garrick's Folly on the other, the event was highly publicized and parodied. Eyewitness accounts ranged widely, some calling it an awe-inspiring event, while others condemned the insipid revelry. Sixty-one years later, the Royal Gala of 1830 was also held in Stratford. It too drew mixed reviews, and it was also soundly satirized. Although the events of the Jubilee have been fairly well recorded and examined, those of the Gala require more consideration and research, particularly since this was the first Stratford celebration to actually include a Shakespearean dramatic performance. I first will consider Garrick's production, suggesting ways in which it may have functioned as a model for Stratford commemorations, before focusing more closely on the Royal Gala half a century later. Like the narrator in Borges' story, we should then 'discover' ways in which these celebrations may conjure up Shakespeare, before choosing to 'accept' or discount this alleged 'memory'.

Garrick's Jubilee[6]

In order to show how the 1769 Jubilee birthed the later ones, specifically the Royal Gala, we will need to revisit the origination and the events of the initial festival. According to most sources, the impetus for a celebration in Shakespeare's home town grew out of a request by the Corporation of Stratford. As the old Town Hall was being rebuilt in 1768, the city elders believed that a donation of some type of monument by Garrick would not only be a fit tribute but also a financial coup, since Garrick would cover any costs of such memorials.[7] In October of that year, therefore, a letter was sent to the 'English Roscius' offering him the title of 'Burgess of Stratford-upon-Avon' and giving him 'freedom of the said borough' enclosed in a 'small neat chest, constructed from the Mulberry-tree, planted by Shakespeare himself'.[8] Garrick's response was predictable. After expressing his 'warmest gratitude', he concluded: 'It would be impossible for me ever to forget those who have honoured me so much, as to mention my unworthy name, with that of their immortal townsman'.[9] The flattery worked; Garrick agreed to supply the town with a memorial, and tentative plans for a September Jubilee were begun in earnest.

First, an amphitheatre was built on Bankcroft, close to the Avon River not far from the present day headquarters of the RSC.[10] The structure was designed to hold upwards of a thousand spectators, and it was also to serve as the location for concerts, feasts, and dances. No expense was spared in the design or in the construction; as Péter Dávidházi observes, the Rotunda was 'meant to resemble both a Roman circus and a church built for the worship of Shakespeare'.[11] Adorned with Corinthian columns, the building also housed a huge, ornate chandelier, consisting of some eight hundred lights. Thirty artillery pieces were placed close by to be fired at the opening of the festivities.[12] Such lavish features of the Jubilee became prototypes for the Shakespeare celebrations to follow.

At approximately five a.m. on Wednesday morning, 6 September, the cannons roared to life, and 'the principal ladies were serenaded under their windows' by young men 'fantastically dressed'.[13] This wake-up performance was followed by a public breakfast at nine, presided over by Garrick. The menu consisted of tea, coffee, and chocolate, and was open to anyone for only a shilling, provided they had also purchased a ticket for at least one of the other entertainments. The hall was filled to overflowing with not only 'the most celebrated beauties of the age, and men distinguished for their wit, genius, and love of the elegant arts', but also persons from the 'meanest situation' in life.[14] While the dining continued, a 'party of drums and fifes performed several pieces opposite the hall, and gave much satisfaction'.[15] This ritual opening of gunfire followed by sweet melodies set the precedent for nearly one hundred years of Stratfordian celebrations.[16]

The group then marched to Holy Trinity Church where more music, including a splendid oratorio, replete with organ music and vocal performances, greeted the guests. After the service ended, Garrick led a 'procession from the church, attended by a large cavalcade of the nobility, and gentry, in their coaches [and] chaises [...] to the amphitheater', loudly singing along the way, 'This is a day, a holiday! a holiday / Drive spleen and rancour far away', for here, the chorus concluded, was where 'Shakspeare walk'd and sung!'.[17] Following the obviously appetite-building procession, another meal was served at 3 p.m., which included 'all the rarities the season could afford'.[18] The first day's events were concluded with fireworks, a ball that ended at midnight, 'at which time the country dances commenced' and three hours later 'all retired'. The whole day, according to this perhaps less-than-objective eyewitness, 'was conducted with the greatest decorum'.[19]

Before proceeding further it would be worthwhile to look at the ways in which this Jubilee functioned as a festive commemoration and also how it affected later Stratfordian celebrations. According to Paul Connerton, borrowing from Steven Lukes, a ritual of remembrance is a 'rule-governed activity of a symbolic character which draws the attention of its participants to objects of thought and feeling which they hold to be of special significance'.[20] Obviously, what Garrick and the planners of the Jubilee hoped to do was to focus the attention of the attendees on Shakespeare as the premier English bard, while also celebrating Stratford as the birthplace of the poet, his own secular 'nativity' scene as one observer called it.[21] It also makes sense that the 'intention' of such events 'is reassurance' while the overall mood is usually 'nostalgic'.[22] These performative events, then, as we shall see, have a unifying purpose. The '[c]ommunity is reminded of its identity as represented by and told in a master narrative', and it seems fair to agree that 'if there is a thing such as social memory, we are likely to find it in commemorative ceremonies'.[23] In many rituals, as Connerton reminds us, 'speech, singing, gesture and dance are bound together in a compositional whole'.[24] This combination of festival events in Stratford, while not wholly without incident, was surely intended by the planners to add up to a 'compositional whole' that in many ways would elevate, if not deify, Shakespeare beyond his mortal status as poet and playwright.[25]

The second day of activities possessed even more characteristics of ritual commemoration as Garrick recited his 'Ode', a verbal monument to Shakespeare's 'memory' written specifically for the event.[26] Although the literary merit of the 'Ode' has been variously debated,[27] Connerton points out that in studying ritual we would be misguided to focus our attention on the content rather than the form of such speech acts, for, as he points out, 'the question as to whether the participants in the rite understand the words is then secondary and is not considered to affect the efficacy of the ritual'.[28] In other words, even for those who did not understand the words of Garrick's 'Ode', not unlike many who listen to a Latin Mass, they could still be moved by the cadences of the speech which would suggest dedication and devotion to Shakespeare.

The meal for the second day was again held at 3 p.m. and was 'numerously attended', but the highlight of this day was the masquerade ball held at midnight.[29] Over 1,000 persons attended, including a slightly inebriated James Boswell dressed as a Corsican pirate 'with pistols in his belt, and a musket at his back'.[30] Perhaps more important for any ritualistic reading, others came clothed as characters from Shakespeare's plays, including the witches from *Macbeth*, Mistress Quickly from *The Merry Wives of Windsor*, and other assorted personages. While this disguising may seem to suggest only sheer amusement, these impersonations may also assume a ritual effect, for 'to wear a mask is to have immediate and direct contact with beings of the unseen world'; so long as they are disguised, the participants 'are not only the representatives of the dead' but they may "become" the ancestors whom these masks portray'.[31] In a Masquerade Ball such as this one, the participants enact 'the idea of bi-presence: the inhabitants of the other world can reappear in this one without leaving their own'.[32] So, those disguised as Shakespeare's characters mix with the more famous folks from the past, and, by doing so, become iconic in their own right. It is also worth remembering that this festive activity would become a central part of the 1830 Gala.

The last day of the festival saw a horse race for the Jubilee Cup just outside of town at Shottery race track. Won by a Mr. Pratt, who confessed he knew very little about plays or Shakespeare, nonetheless it was well attended and offered much 'diversion to lovers of the turf'.[33] More dancing occurred that evening and the highlight, according to many accounts, was a minuet performed by Mrs. Garrick.

What I want to trace now is how the events of this first Shakespeare commemoration served as a prototype for many that followed, particularly the Royal Gala of 1830. For although these 'invented traditions' in Eric Hobsbawm's words, 'claim to be old' as well as authentic, they are usually neither, but more likely to be 'quite recent in origin' and 'invented [and] constructed' and only then 'formally instituted'.[34]

The Royal Gala of 1830

Between Garrick's Jubilee and the Royal Gala one other celebration was held in Stratford. In 1827 the first festival actually held on 'the Natal Day of Shakespeare' and the 'King's adopted birth-day' (23–27 April) allowed the participants not only 'the opportunity of testifying their unalterable attachment to their King; but, at the same time, of paying tribute of respect to the memory of their illustrious Townsman'.[35] The three-day event followed the pattern of Garrick's festival – with speeches, processions, music, and balls. In fact, due to similarities in the 'performative structure' of these Shakespearean celebrations, like all invented rituals, they 'rapidly assumed a canonical form'.[36]

The planning for the 1830 Gala was begun immediately following the 1827 event, and 'it was decided that the forth-coming Pageant should be brought out upon as brilliant and extensive a scale as possible'.[37] In addition, like the 1827 commemoration, but unlike Garrick's celebration (he had been too busy to present the Jubilee in April), the festivities would be held on the poet's birthday, for as Connerton points out, 'rituals tend to occur at special places at fixed times', in recurrent calendrical ceremonies, such as 'those associated with birth'.[38] For the Planning Committee it must have been quite symbolic that they could not only celebrate both the birthday and burial day of Shakespeare, but also got to throw in the King's adopted birthday for good measure as well as St George's. In fact, Robert Peel petitioned the King himself to join in the patronage of the festival, and the King, 'himself a lover and indefatigable fosterer of Literature and the Fine Arts', readily assented.[39] Thus literary royalty was wedded to political royalty and, as others have pointed out, the Stratford celebrations took on a nationalistic if not nation-building component.[40]

By examining three events of the 1830 Gala, we will see how the ritualistic aspects of the Garrick celebration were developed even further and acquired a sense of accretion that is still visible today. The first day of the celebration, as with the prototype, was begun by 'the customary firing of cannon',[41] and by '9 o'clock all the roads leading to the town were thronged with people, some on foot, others on horseback, and carriages of every description'.[42] The single most important event of the first day was the Dramatic Procession that took place at 2 p.m. Gathering at the newly constructed pavilion, over one hundred and fifty costumed participants fell in line behind the leader of the procession, a Mr. Ashfield, on 'horseback, attired in the dress of a Chief Constable in Queen Elizabeth's time'.[43] A large band came next and then 'The Committee of the Shakspearean Club'. Charles Kean representing St George, 'seated on a grey horse' and 'clad in a complete suit of polished steel armour' followed wearing a steel helmet adorned with 'ostrich feathers'.[44]

Numerous characters from Shakespeare's plays marched next in the procession, all grouped according to the production from which they were freed – Julius Caesar, the Witches from *Macbeth*, Romeo and Juliet, Falstaff, Prospero, and over seventy-five more, some on horseback, some walking – creating, in essence, a 'quasi-textual representation'.[45] All of the individuals, according to this official narrative, 'seemed animated by a true dramatic feeling: and the beauty, richness and strict classical propriety of the varied costumes [...] were beyond all praise'.[46] When the procession arrived in Henley Street, they ascended to a temporary stage built in front of Shakespeare's birthplace, where 'every inch of ground [was] covered with spectators, the windows and house-tops were full, and every possible resting place occupied'.[47] Thus, it seems fair to credit Garrick's masquerade ball as the prototype for this much more extravagant production, a proliferation of publicly displayed Shakespearean characters and various theatrical icons, including the muses of tragedy and comedy.[48] More significant is that the porousness of the parade enabled onlookers to participate in the pageantry by mingling with the marchers and thus helped to promote Shakespeare's literary fame and status not only as national hero but also as a local one.

Equally important, if we believe that systems of clothing can suggest structures of language, apparel may become the materialization 'of the main co-ordinates of person and occasion', and if so, can also be interpreted as a 'complex scheme of cultural categories and the relations between them'.[49] In this Pageant, for example, both English Royalty and Shakespeare's characters are blended with real politicians, dignitaries, and assorted members from the Shakespeare Committee to form a pious parade representing the King, Shakespeare, and the English Nation. Moreover, since costuming 'is decodeable at a glance' by the spectators, 'it works at an unconscious level, the conception being built into visual perception itself', so much so that clothing not only conveys messages but may also influence behaviour.[50] Perhaps the decorum of costume and occasion did help to shape the behaviour of the townspeople, because even though constables were hired 'at a great expense' to keep the 'town clear of bad characters' it turned out that not a single incident 'occurred to mar the general joy'.[51] Dinner and dancing followed the Pageant as it did at the Jubilee.

Inserted into this festival narrative, however, we find an interesting, albeit brief note for Day One: 'The Theatre also attracted an overflowing audience to witness the performance of Mr. Kean, Jun.'[52] After twenty pages devoted to the Procession, this seems scant description, a point to which I will return below; and recent scholarship has discovered that it was not even a Shakespearean play that was performed that night on Shakespeare's birthday.[53]

The second day's events followed a similar pattern to Garrick's, a breakfast, followed by a concert, which was preceded by a recitative Ode ala Garrick's, which concluded with the following musical 'GRAND FINALE': 'Hail! to Shakespeare's magic strain / "we ne'er shall look upon his like again"'.[54] In the evening, another 'Masquerade and Fancy-Ball' was held at the pavilion, and like Garrick's, people came costumed in various disguises, from Charles the Second, to Othello, to the fool from *Lear*. At the close of the account another brief mention of a Shakespearean performance is noted: 'The Theatre again attracted a numerous and respectable audience – Mr. Kean, Jun. displayed considerable ability, and already stood high in the general favour: the other performers respectably supported the parts allotted to them'.[55] And that is that. No mention of the play title or any type of critique in this official narrative.[56]

Another characteristic of ritual commemoration occurred during the third day's events, the toasts and speeches given at the public dinner at the White Lion Hotel held at 4 p.m. Recalling that speech acts are 'predictable' since 'there is only one appropriate sequence along which one can properly proceed', we will now consider the language as well as the non-verbal signs of such acts.[57] While many other meals, as we have seen, were open to the public, this dinner seems to have been by invitation only and just over 100 'gentlemen' sat down to the 'elegant and abundant repast'.[58] The toasts began with one to the King, followed by '*loud and reiterated applause*'; the next to the Duke of Clarence, and the rest of the Royal Family, followed by '*Continued cheers*'; and the third to 'The Immortal Memory of Shakespeare'. This was followed by no cheers. Instead, those present '[d]rank in solemn silence'.⁵⁹ If we measure status by these opening toasts, we can already hear how the invocation of Shakespeare's name trumps even royalty in the respect afforded it.

After toasts to various other patrons, concluding with one to the Mayor of Stratford (which was followed by '*immense cheering*'), the Mayor rose to give his speech.⁶⁰ He began by thanking the attendees for honouring him with a toast, and also recalled how the Royal Gala itself had his 'warmest sanction'. He concluded his presentation by praising the 'Dramatic Procession' as one 'worthy of the *Poet*, and of the Royal and distinguished patronage it had previously received'.⁶¹ Connerton is again helpful in assessing the ritualistic aspects of such behaviour, for as he notes, 'speech acts of different participants are determined in advance; from the speech act of one participant one can predict that of the next', for in the many speeches that follow, we observe ritualized 'posture, gesture and movement'.⁶² For example, Mr. Raymond presented to the group a 'beautiful rich cut-glass goblet' described as 'a very splendid specimen' from a Mr. Cheesman, a 'genuine' lover of Shakespeare who could not be present that afternoon.⁶³ When we consider the feasting and drinking, and now with the introduction of a sacred goblet into the proceedings, the religious as well as ritualistic aspects of the dinner come into sharper focus.

This sacred symbolism is best summed up in the last speech of the afternoon. Mr. Wilkins, a 'genuine admirer of the Poet' who had been 'strenuously exerting himself to establish a Branch Shakspearean Club at Birmingham' rose to 'express in common' with all 'genuine votaries' of Shakespeare his own 'admiration' of Shakespeare's 'talents'.⁶⁴ Today, he proclaimed, those assembled had performed 'a duty to Heaven' and to their 'country', explaining,

> A duty to Heaven, inasmuch as you are testifying your gratitude to an All-wise Providence for having blessed you with such a man as the Immortal Shakspeare; and a duty to your Country, because you are shewing [sic] a proper feeling of admiration for a Poet, the pride and glory of his native land, and the envy of the whole world.⁶⁵

Word, ritual, nation, poet, and God – all combined to provide an evocation to Shakespeare's marvellous being, and he ends his toast to the 'veneration' of Shakespeare's 'memory'.⁶⁶ Clearly, this assembled group of devotees not only accepted Shakespeare's memory but clasped it to their hearts in a semi-sacred embrace.

The Gala continued with a ball that evening, another performance, and the narrative includes a bit more description of Kean's acting, claiming that he 'gave evident proofs of his rising talent'; yet there is still no mention of the play itself nor any account of the other performers or even the audience's reaction, although Isabel Roome Mann speculates that it was Kean playing in *Hamlet* that night.[67]

The fourth day was fairly anti-climatic according to most accounts; the pageant was partly repeated and in the evening there was a ball at Shakespeare's Hall. As the narrator notes, the evening was concluded by 'a masquerade, fireworks, and a performance at the theatre', the drama noted again but without details. On the following day, the pavilion was closed, although little children were provided 'gratuitous admission' in order to 'view the internal decorations'.[68] This official narrative concludes with a nod to the 'small but patriotic band of men, [who] have raised up a spirit in their native town, which will, perhaps, never be destroyed'.[69] This 'suffering' of the little children to visit the now sacred shrine and the nod to eternal English patriotism conclude the Gala account.

But what are we to make of the short shrift given to the actual plays performed at the Gala, and how did this festival serve as a pivotal one in the Stratford celebrations? We have already hinted at the notion that Shakespeare as a playwright in some way needed to be transcended. Michael Dobson suggests that the attendees, in fact, were not unlike the tourists who now stream to Stratford and its sites, but never consider viewing a play.[70] We also should recall that in 1830, acting was still considered by many to be a less than decorous occupation, although Kean himself tried tirelessly to change this throughout his lifetime.[71] What we do know is that for the 1864 Tercentenary, Charles Flower, the brewer, funded a huge, wooden stage for performances,[72] close to what is now the Courtyard Theatre, and a total of four plays were performed during this celebration: *Twelfth Night, Romeo and Juliet, The Comedy of Errors,* and *As You Like It*.[73] Each night, according to George Morley, 'a goodly company of apostles assembled to do homage to the memory of Shakespeare'.[74] In these instances, however, the tribute to Shakespeare focused as much on his plays as on his person. This trend, then, begun at the 1830 Gala, was the first to combine theatre and tourism, even if the official narrative of the time failed to recognize its importance. It may even be fair to say that the Jubilee and the Gala represent the twin pillars of the Shakespeare industry today.

Epilogue

In Borges' story with which we began, Professor Sörgel tries to coax Shakespeare's memory to surface more quickly once he has accepted it. To accomplish this feat, he pours over Shakespeare's sources, rereads the Sonnets, and journeys to Stratford. Yet, the trip to the birthplace was 'predictable enough' even 'sterile', according to Sörgel, producing no new recollections.[75] More significantly, he soon comes to realize that Shakespeare's 'fables' and the characters he created were 'much more alive than the gray man who dreamed them'.[76] In other words, the imagination and the art of Shakespeare should be considered as much as the man who possessed and produced it. Unfortunately, it took 100 years and three major Shakespearean celebrations for the planners of Stratford commemorations to reach a similar conclusion.[77]

Robert Sawyer is Professor of English at East Tennessee State University, where he teaches Shakespeare, Victorian Literature, and Literary Criticism. Author of *Victorian Appropriations of Shakespeare* (Fairleigh Dickinson UP, 2003), he is also co-editor of *Shakespeare and Appropriation* (Routledge, 1999), and *Harold Bloom's Shakespeare* (Palgrave, 2001). His book entitled *Marlowe and Shakespeare: The Critical Rivalry* was published by Palgrave in 2017, and the same press also published his latest monograph, *Shakespeare between the World Wars: The Anglo-American Sphere* in 2019.

Notes

1. Jorge Luis Borges, 'Shakespeare's Memory', in *Collected Fictions*, trans. Andrew Hurley (New York: Viking, 1998), 510.
2. 'Shakespeare's Memory', 511.
3. 'Shakespeare's Memory', 512.
4. 'Shakespeare's Memory', 513–14.
5. 'Shakespeare's Memory', 515.
6. Christian Deelman's *The Great Shakespeare Jubilee* (New York: Viking, 1964) is the most comprehensive book on the Jubilee. Chapter 5 of Michael Dobson's *The Making of the National Poet: Shakespeare, Adaptation and Authorship, 1660–1769* (Oxford: Oxford University Press, 1992) was particularly helpful on the Jubilee and the emerging notions of English Bardolatry. Also see Martha W. England, *Garrick's Jubilee* (Columbus: Ohio State Press, 1964), and Péter Dávidházi, *The Romantic Cult of Shakespeare: Literary Reception in Anthropological Perspective* (London: Macmillan, 1998), chapter 2.

7. Garrick eventually donated both a statue and a painting of Shakespeare, and he also commissioned a painting of himself.
8. *Stratford and Antiquities of Stratford-upon-Avon: comprising a description of the collegiate church, the life of Shakespeare, and copies of several documents relating to him and his family, never before printed; with a biographical sketch of other eminent characters, natives of, or who have resided in Stratford. To which is added, a particular account of the jubilee, celebrated at Stratford, in honour of our immortal bard* (London: J. Ward, 1806), 166.
9. *Stratford and Antiquities of Stratford-upon-Avon*, 166.
10. Dobson, *The Making of the National Poet*, 226n6.
11. Dávidházi, *The Romantic Cult of Shakespeare*, 38.
12. *Stratford and Antiquities of Stratford-upon-Avon*, 168.
13. *Stratford and Antiquities of Stratford-upon-Avon*, 169.
14. *Stratford and Antiquities of Stratford-upon-Avon*, 171.
15. *Stratford and Antiquities of Stratford-upon-Avon*, 171–72.
16. Robert Hunter, *Shakespeare and Stratford-upon-Avon. 'A Chronicle of the Time'* (London: Whittaker and Co., 1864), 166. The 1864 Tercentenary, according to witnesses, began with an 'ominous quietude throughout the streets', no 'cannon, bands or bells were to be heard'. That the narrator even comments on this absence suggests just how ritualistic the noisy opening ceremonies had become.
17. *Stratford and Antiquities of Stratford-upon-Avon*, 172.
18. *Stratford and Antiquities of Stratford-upon-Avon*, 173.
19. *Stratford and Antiquities of Stratford-upon-Avon*, 173.
20. Paul Connerton, *How Societies Remember* (Cambridge: Cambridge University Press, 1989), 44.
21. *Stratford and Antiquities of Stratford-upon-Avon*, 163.
22. Connerton, *How Societies Remember*, 64.
23. Connerton, *How Societies Remember*, 71.
24. Connerton, *How Societies Remember*, 60.
25. It should be remembered that not a single part of any Shakespearean play was included in the Jubilee celebration. For a more jaundiced view of the Jubilee, see Brooks McNamara, 'The Stratford Jubilee: Dram to Garrick's Vanity', *Educational Theatre Journal* 14:2 (May 1962), 125–30.
26. *Stratford and Antiquities of Stratford-upon-Avon*, 174.
27. Eyewitnesses claimed that the 'elegant Ode' was met with 'the most universal approbation and applause' (*Stratford and Antiquities of Stratford-upon-Avon*, 185), while McNamara refers to it as 'dubiously poetic' ('The Stratford Jubilee', 138). In any case, Dobson is certainly correct to call it an 'invocation of the national spirit' (*The Making of the National Poet*, 218).
28. Connerton, *How Societies Remember*, 67.
29. *Stratford and Antiquities of Stratford-upon-Avon*, 188.
30. *Stratford and Antiquities of Stratford-upon-Avon*, 189.
31. Connerton, *How Societies Remember*, 69.
32. Connerton, *How Societies Remember*, 69.
33. *Stratford and Antiquities of Stratford-upon-Avon*, 190.
34. Eric Hobsbawm, 'Introduction', in *The Invention of Tradition*, ed. Eric Hobsbawm and Terence Ranger (Cambridge: Cambridge University Press, 1983), 1.
35. *A Descriptive Account of the Second Royal Gala Festival at Stratford-upon-Avon* (Stratford-upon-Avon: R. Lapworth, 1830), 1, 11.
36. Connerton, *How Societies Remember*, 41.

37. *Descriptive Account*, 17.
38. Connerton, *How Societies Remember*, 44.
39. *Descriptive Account*, 17.
40. See Dobson, *The Making of the National Poet*, 218–22; Jonathan Bate, *The Genius of Shakespeare* (Oxford: Oxford University Press, 1998), 169; and Coppélia Kahn, 'Remembering Shakespeare Imperially: The 1916 Tercentenary', *Shakespeare Quarterly* 52:4 (Winter 2001), 456–78.
41. Hunter, *Shakespeare and Stratford-upon-Avon*, 81.
42. *Descriptive Account*, 18.
43. *Descriptive Account*, 20.
44. *Descriptive Account*, 21.
45. Connerton, *How Societies Remember*, 49.
46. *Descriptive Account*, 30.
47. *Descriptive Account*, 30.
48. Many would argue that the Jubilee itself was more a celebration of Garrick than Shakespeare, and since the 1830 Gala had less egotistical leaders, the Bard became more central to the celebration.
49. Connerton, *How Societies Remember*, 33.
50. Connerton, *How Societies Remember*, 33.
51. *Descriptive Account*, 38.
52. *Descriptive Account*, 65.
53. Isabel Roome Mann, 'The Royal Gala of 1830', *Shakespeare Quarterly* 14:3 (Summer, 1963), 263–6. Mann has uncovered playbills that reveal that the play was Philip Massinger's *A New Way to Pay Old Debts*, starring Kean as Sir Giles Overreach (265). *Descriptive Account*, 73.
54. *Descriptive Account*, 70.
55. *Descriptive Account*, 81.
56. Mann suggests that the play was *Richard III*, starring Kean in the title role (265).
57. Connerton, *How Societies Work*, 60.
58. *Descriptive Account*, 75.
59. *Descriptive Account*, 75.
60. *Descriptive Account*, 76.
61. *Descriptive Account*, 76.
62. Connerton, *How Societies Work*, 60–61.
63. *Descriptive Account*, 76–77.
64. *Descriptive Account*, 78–79.
65. *Descriptive Account*, 79.
66. *Descriptive Account*, 79.
67. Mann, 'The Royal Gala of 1830', 266.
68. *Descriptive Account*, 87.
69. *Descriptive Account*, 87.
70. Dobson, *The Making of the National Poet*, 226.
71. See Robert Sawyer, 'Introduction' to *Lives of Shakesperian Actors Vol 1: Charles Kean*, ed. Robert Sawyer (London: Pickering and Chatto, 2010), xvii-xxvi.
72. George Morley, *Round Shakespeare's Table: An Account of the Birthday Celebrations held at Stratford-on-Avon in honour of the Poet* (Birmingham: The Midland Counties Herald Limited, 1908), 40. Morley describes the stage as seventy-four feet long by fifty-six feet wide, with seating for close to 4,000 patrons, half in the galleries.
73. The best account of this festival is Foulkes (1984); also see Foulkes (1997). Richard

Foulkes, *Church and Stage in Victorian England* (Cambridge: Cambridge University Press, 1989) and ibid., *The Shakespeare Tercentenary of 1864* (London: The Society for Theatre Research, 1984).
74. Morley, *Round Shakespeare's Table*, 40.
75. Borges, 'Shakespeare's Memory', 512.
76. 'Shakespeare's Memory', 514.
77. I want to thank the Marco Institute at the University of Tennessee for a Visiting Fellowship in 2010 which allowed me access to the rare book holdings in the John C. Hodges Library at the University of Tennessee.

Chapter 4
Shakespeare Remembered[1]

Graham Holderness

> My theme is memory [...] for we possess nothing certainly except the past. – Evelyn Waugh, *Brideshead Revisited*

In the heart of the city lies a garden: *hortus in urbe*.[2] Not far from the ruins of London's ancient city walls; close to the Guildhall, former seat of London's civic power; just round the corner from where Shakespeare used to lodge in Silver Street, a tiny space among the clutter of buildings marks out the site of the mediaeval church of St Mary the Virgin, Aldermanbury. Only the 'footprint' of the church remains. Some paved brick elevations, a bit of grass and a few trees, a couple of benches: just a pleasant spot for a tired city worker to sit for a while and drink his cappuccino. But the tiny garden is dominated by a granite memorial, dating from 1896, flanked about with inscribed bronze plaques, and surmounted by a bust of Shakespeare. Only indirectly, however, is it a memorial to Shakespeare, since it explicitly commemorates the lives of two men who dwelt in the parish, worshipped and officiated in the church, and are buried in the former churchyard: John Heminge and Henry Condell, editors of the First Folio.[3]

The monument, which was originally erected in the centre of the churchyard, was unveiled by the Lord Mayor of London on 15 July 1896, in a ceremony attended by the American Ambassador and Sir

Notes for this section begin on page 61.

Henry Irving. The plinth is constructed of Aberdeen red granite, the plaques and the bust of bronze. The head of Shakespeare is modelled on the bust in Holy Trinity Church, Stratford, and the Droeshout engraving.[4] Underneath the bust is a pale grey granite representation of an open book, which looks at first sight like that typical feature of a Victorian gravestone, the book recording the name of the deceased and inscribed with an epitaph. These granite pages however commemorate not some dear departed's book of life, but an actual book, the 1623 First Folio. One page displays the Folio title, the other an edited extract from Heminge and Condell's dedication to the earls of Pembroke and Montgomery:

> We have but collected them, and done an office to the dead ... without ambition either of selfe-profit, or fame; onely to keepe the memory of so worthy a Friend, & Fellow aliue, as was our S H A K E S P E A R E ...
>
>   IOHN HEMINGE.
>   HENRY CONDELL.

The full text in its original context reads:

> We have but collected them, and done an office to the dead, to procure his Orphanes, Guardians; without ambition either of selfe-profit, or fame: onely to keepe the memory of so worthy a Friend, & Fellow alive, as was our S H A K E S P E A R E, by humble offer of his playes, to your most noble patronage.[5]

The abridged version on the monument deletes the patrons, and effaces the context of patronage. Nothing here is owing to the memories of the Earls of Pembroke and Montgomery. The edited quotation dwells rather on the disinterested and charitable work of the editors Heminge and Condell in collecting and publishing the plays, their conception of the First Folio as a memorial tribute, or even a funeral elegy (an 'office to the dead'), and their intention of keeping Shakespeare's name alive in the public memory. The bronze plaques on the four sides of the monument (numbered here 1 to 4, starting with the 'front' of the monument and working clockwise round the plinth) thus commemorate the editors, along with the author, of the First Folio. Plaque 3 commemorates Heminge and Condell in the manner of a funeral monument, indicating that they and their families lived in the parish and are buried there.[6] Plaque 2 presents an extract from their prefatory 'Address to the Great Variety of Readers'.

Beneath the stone Folio that clearly marks the 'front' of the monument, the primary commemorative page, Plaque 1, links Heminge and Condell together with Shakespeare:

> To the memory of JOHN HEMINGE and HENRY CONDELL, fellow actors and personal friends of SHAKESPEARE. They lived many years in this parish and are buried here.
>
> To their disinterested affection the world owes all that it calls SHAKESPEARE.[7] They alone collected his dramatic writings, regardless of pecuniary loss and without the hope of any profit, gave them to the world.
>
> THEY THUS MERITED THE GRATITUDE OF MANKIND.

Plaque 4 however further commemorates Heminge and Condell as primarily responsible for the survival of Shakespeare's work, the world indebted to them for 'all that it calls Shakespeare':

> The fame of Shakespeare rests on his incomparable dramas. There is no evidence that he ever intended to publish them and his premature death in 1616 made this the interest of no one else. HEMINGE AND CONDELL had been co-partners with him in the Globe Theatre Southwark and from the accumulated plays there of thirty-five years with great labour selected them. No men then living were so competent having acted with him in them for many years and well knowing his manuscript, they were published in 1623 in Folio, thus giving away their private rights therein. What they did was priceless, for the whole of his manuscripts with almost all those of the dramas of the period have perished.

'We remember Heminge and Condell', wrote Laurie Maguire, 'because they remembered Shakespeare'.[8] The Aldermanbury monument states the absolute opposite: we would not remember Shakespeare if Heminge and Condell had not taken the trouble to remember him. 'Though crowned by a bust of Shakespeare', writes Philip Ward Jackson, 'it is not he who is commemorated, but the men who gathered his *opus* together after his death and presented it to the world in the First Folio edition'.[9] Without these facilitators, the work would have been lost forever. Culture is the bequest of the editor, rather than of the poet.

This position was fully developed in an associated book, privately published in 1896 by the man responsible for funding, commissioning, and designing the monument, Charles Clement Walker.[10] Walker was a Midlands industrialist, manager of the ironworks at Donnington in Shropshire, a respected philanthropist who established reading rooms and baths for his workers, and an amateur enthusiast for Shakespeare. The Vestry Minutes of St Mary Aldermanbury for 31 July 1895 contain a transcript of Walker's formal application to erect the monument at the church, and show that other sites had been considered, such as Blackfriars and Southwark 'where Shakespeare's works were first published'. But the parish of St Mary was considered more appropriate, since Heminge and Condell were buried there.

Walker explains that his motivation for installing the monument was a strong sense that Heminge and Condell were hidden in Shakespeare's giant shadow, their names unknown to all but Shakespeare scholars. To commemorate them should have been a public duty, and the monument erected by public subscription, but since they remained unknown, he had to step in to correct this injustice:

> Without doubt a memorial to these men should have been raised by public subscription, but wide inquiry showed that while Shakespearian scholars well knew their merits and how much mankind owe to them, their names are almost unknown to the generality of readers; and of their merits, not one in a thousand of English-speaking men was conscious.[11]

This is not as it should be, since among public benefactors worthy of monuments

> [...] none are more worthy to be commemorated than Heminge and Condell, to whom alone the world is indebted for this first edition of what it calls 'Shakespeare'. Their own story of the reasons which moved them to publish this collection is such a beautiful instance of unselfishness, singular love of Shakespeare, and unaffected modesty, that the writer felt it only needed to become well understood by the public for their merits to be appreciated. The most certain way to bring about this desirable result was to erect a monument to Heminge and Condell to be before the public eye.[12]

The monument then celebrates Shakespeare's work, rather than Shakespeare himself. Walker had no doubts about the value of that work, and the importance of its preservation and transmission to posterity. He alludes to, but dismisses, the Shakespeare authorship controversy, at that time focused on Francis Bacon, on the grounds that the plays could only have been written by a man of the theatre.[13] He concedes, on the other hand, that the genesis of the work from the life of 'the Stratford man' remains hard to explain. No mystery however surrounds the process via which the works were secured for posterity: 'while we are unable fully to explain their production in such circumstances as developed Shakespeare, we have no such difficulty in showing to whom we are indebted for the preservation of his writings'.[14] Shakespeare's works are a 'treasure', produced, like precious minerals from the earth, by a process we cannot fully understand. But our access to that treasure depends absolutely on the good offices of the 'treasure-keepers', Heminge and Condell:

> It is now nearly three centuries since the volume we call 'Shakespeare' appeared before the world. Age has not dimmed its brightness; Time has proved its pre-eminence. There is probably no other masterpiece of literature which in the circumstances of its evolution has had a more remarkable history; and for the possession of this treasure we are indebted to [...] John Heminge and Henry Condell.[15]

The Aldermanbury monument is a strangely hybrid construction, with multiple and at first sight discontinuous commemorative functions. It looks like a tombstone, with its open volume and lapidary inscriptions, and functions as such in relation to Heminge and Condell, who were both buried in the churchyard. Plaque 3 memorializes their names and other details from the parish records, in exactly the manner of a gravestone. On the other hand, the head that caps the monument is of course that of another, Shakespeare, whose name also appears on the plinth. In this dimension the monument looks more heroic than funereal, and the dark bronze bust, foreshortened as one looks up, frowns down at the viewer rather as does Karl Marx's head in Highgate Cemetery. At this point the red granite column, with its rectangular bronze plaques bearing a pointed recollection of those not to be forgotten names, begins to look more like a war memorial. Red granite was used for some memorials set up in the 1850s in memory of the Crimean War,[16] and the polished stone plinth, with its sequence of plaques around the column, became the standard form for the war memorials that were established in or adjoining most English churches after the First World War. Heminge and Condell belong to those who are 'fallen', not in war but in time, and are here piously and reverently commemorated, 'lest we forget'.

This dimension of the Aldermanbury monument is apposite, since the garden in which it stands is itself a war memorial. Site of a church from as early as the twelfth century (the garden preserves the bases of some mediaeval columns), St Mary's was destroyed in the Great Fire, and was one of the fourteen churches that began construction in 1670 under the rebuilding programme of Christopher Wren.[17] Wren's church stood until engulfed in a second conflagration, Dr Goebbels' 'Second Great Fire of London', the Blitz of 1940, when its roof was struck by an incendiary bomb and the building partially destroyed, only the walls left standing. On this occasion there was no Wren to undertake the rebuilding. In the aftermath of the war, British authorities assessed the destruction inflicted by enemy bombing and debated whether severely damaged buildings should be rebuilt, demolished, or preserved. Churches in particular, as homes for worshipping communities, seemed to call for reconstruction; but some were damaged beyond repair, or could be rebuilt only at substantial expense. The Ministry of Town and Country Planning held that churches should not be rebuilt unless they were of significant architectural merit, or not too badly damaged. St Mary's however was a church designed by Wren, and the Bishop of London's 1941 commission ruled that that 'no Wren church, not already destroyed, nor damaged beyond the possibility of satisfactory restoration, should be removed, except in a case of most urgent necessity, and after all the schemes for entire or partial preservation have been fully considered'.[18]

An alternative to rebuilding was to leave the bombed churches in their state of ruination, particularly in the City of London, as mute but eloquent testimonies to the violence that destroyed them. Such memorials would be at once beautiful, provocative of thought, and of practical use to City workers. Ruined buildings could function as 'memory-bearing' sites, housing or even becoming war memorials, testimonies to a violence and injustice that should not be forgotten. Architectural historian John Summerson argued that if a church was not needed as a place of worship, 'why not let it remain as a shell, a witness – and a beautiful one – of the acts of these times as well as of its own'.[19] The idea was floated in the *Architectural Review* in January 1944, and a letter appeared in the *Times* on 15 August of the same year, under the heading 'Ruined City Churches', and signed by leading cultural figures such as Kenneth Clark, Julian Huxley, Lord

Keynes, David Cecil, architect H.S. Goodhart-Rendel, and T.S. Eliot. Churches that had been very severely damaged should not be either restored in an inappropriate pastiche of their former style, or replaced by an entirely new building, but be left as they stood: 'preserved in their true condition, as permanent memorials of this war'. In a relatively short time, the proposers predicted, the City would be rebuilt, and no trace of the prime battlefield of the Home Front would remain.

> The time will come [...] when no trace of death from the air will be left in the streets of rebuilt London. At such a time the story of the Blitz may begin to seem unreal not only to visiting tourists but to a new generation of Londoners.

Whilst serving as sites of relaxation and meditation in the heart of the city, such churches would also fulfil the prime function of a memorial: 'to remind posterity of the reality of the sacrifices upon which its apparent security has been built'.[20]

This position was fully developed in a booklet, *Bombed Churches as War Memorials*, published by the Architectural Press (1945).[21] This built upon the *Architectural Review* piece, using many of the same illustrations, and reprinted as its frontispiece 'Ruined City Churches' from *The Times*. Introduced by Hugh Casson, it contained detailed proposals for Christ Church, Newgate, and other bombed churches in London. Casson's essay bears the Shakespearean title, 'Ruins for Remembrance', and advocates preservation of the ruins as sanctuaries, open spaces, and war memorials. Even in ruins, churches can disclose 'significance', 'nobility' and 'great beauty'.[22]

> They are aloof, but have not lost contact with us, and with us they have undergone the physical trials of war, and bear its scars. But though they stand today upon what is still a battle-field, it will not always be so. It will be many years before all traces of war damage will have gone, and its strange beauty vanished from our streets. No longer will the evening sky be seen reflected in the water-pools which today lie dark and quiet between the torn and gaping walls. Soon a pock-marked parapet or a broken cornice will be to future generations the only signs of former shock and flame.[23] The shabby heaps of stones, flowering with willow-herb as pink and lively as the flames which earlier sprouted from their crevices, will disappear, and with their going the ordeal through which we passed will seem remote, unreal, perhaps forgotten.

'A church like St Mary's', Casson argued,

stands, even when in ruins, upon sacred ground. It is, even when scarred and broken, a piece of architecture, sometimes perhaps a masterpiece. Every stone – whether fallen or in place – is a fragment of the past, part of the pattern of history. To destroy all this just because it was in the way, or because on Sunday the pews were mostly empty, is surely indefensible, however many new churches are built elsewhere to take its place.[24]

St Mary's remained in this condition, as an open-air 'chapel of ease' for prayer and meditation, for some twenty years.[25] In the earlier consultations the Ministry of Town and Country Planning had suggested that some churches might be removed and relocated, freeing up inner-city space for redevelopment. In the case of St Mary's Aldermanbury, this happened, some time later, with a vengeance. When Westminster College asked for a ruined church to be transported to Fulton, Missouri, to build a memorial to Sir Winston Churchill, the diocese of London gave them St Mary's. The ruins of the church were in 1966 transported to America, and a simulacrum of Wren's church rebuilt using the reclaimed bricks. In their history of the church Hauer and Young call it a 'phoenix' rising from the ashes of two major conflagrations.[26]

Back in London the empty 'footprint' of the church became the Aldermanbury garden, which preserves only a few stumps of fifteenth-century columns left after the Great Fire, and the Aldermanbury monument to Heminge and Condell. The longer history of the church and its double destruction is memorialized in a slate tablet installed by Westminster College. 'Aldermanbury Gardens' is thus a site of commemoration on a number of different levels. It recalls a mediaeval church destroyed by fire and a Restoration reconstruction ruined by another flame. It is a memorial to the Second World War and the massive violence and suffering inflicted on the civilian population of Britain by enemy bombing. And it is a garden of remembrance for Shakespeare, his editors, and their joint publication the First Folio.[27] Thus it combines the functions of heritage site, war memorial, cemetery, and library, all in one.

Do these separate functions really hang together? To some extent the various features of the garden seem to cohere only accidentally, a random collection of contingent objects and traces that happen to have found themselves in the same place. The mediaeval columns are, literally and metaphorically, broken off from their history. Wren's church has been given away. Few people using the gardens would be aware that it was once a 'Ground Zero' marking a past atrocity. And the statue of Shakespeare now seems oddly out of place, as if it would have been better located in Southwark, where the reconstructed Globe now stands, or in the theatre district of the West End, like the statue of Shakespeare in Leicester Square. Walker claimed that it was the only public bust of Shakespeare to be erected inside the City of London, and this may well still be the case.[28] The City certainly didn't want Shakespeare's theatre when it was active and alive, so there seems no good reason why it should want to remember him dead.

In another sense the monument is less about the author and his editors as it is about the book, the First Folio. The material presence of the book itself gives form to the structure.[29]

The book is there, openly displayed for the observer to read. It is there in the bronze plaques that resemble pages, one of them duplicating an actual page from the Folio. It is there in the monument's commemoration of the men responsible for its publication. Like an empty tomb that encloses only the memory of its incumbent, the monument inscribes the presence of the departed in literary form, combining the memorial capacities of sepulchre and book. John Weever's definition of a monument recognized the parallel capacities of monument and book to act as memorials:

> A Monument is a thing erected, made, or written, for a memorial of some remarkable action, fit to be transferred to future posterities [...]. Now aboue all remembrances (by which men haue endeuoured, euen in despight of death to giue vnto their Fames eternitie) for worthinesse and continuance, bookes, or writings, haue euer had the preheminence ...[30]

This process of mementifying the book as proxy for the author's fame is clearly operating at several removes, since the First Folio was itself so pointedly a memorial tribute to the author Shakespeare. The dedication is defined as 'an office to the dead', and throughout it echoes the language of the burial service: *'we most humbly consecrate to your H. H. these remaines of your servant Shakespeare ...'* The address 'To the Great Variety of Readers' makes it clear that the editors saw themselves as executors to a will, undertaking on behalf of the deceased the tasks he himself was prevented by death from fulfilling. The gathering of the works on behalf of the author announces his constitutive absence from the process, and renders the act of publication a posthumous service of commemoration. Heminge and Condell then extend this figure to suggest that in collecting the works the editors are in one sense reconstructing the author 'by death departed', piecing back together the fragments dispersed by time and corruption. Here the plays are presented 'cur'd and perfect of their limbs', as if in the process the body of the author is being restored, even resurrected.

> It had bene a thing, we confesse, worthie to have bene wished, that the Author himself had liv'd to have set forth, and overseen his owne writings; But since it hath bin ordain'd otherwise, and he by death departed from that right, we pray you do not envie his Friends, the office of their care, and paine, to have collected & publish'd them; and so to have publish'd them, as where (before) you were abus'd with diverse stolne, and surreptitious copies, maimed, and deformed by the frauds and stealthes of injurious impostors, that expos'd them: even those, are now offer'd to your view cur'd, and perfect of their limbes; and all the rest, absolute in their numbers, as he conceived the[m].

As Laurie Maguire puts it, deploying the pun that supplies my title, the editors 'not only remember Shakespeare, they literally re-member him', using a 'language of embalmment', and an 'anthropomorphising vocabulary' in which plays are conceived, maimed, deformed, cured, and furnished with limbs.[31] The Folio, says Maguire 'is both a relic of the deceased and a memorial to him'.[32] She quotes John Weever's more literal definition of a funeral monument as 'a receptacle or sepulchre, purposely made, erected, or built, to receiue a dead corps, and to preserue the same from violation'.[33] The Folio was designed to contain the corpus of the author's writings, both to retain memory of them and to preserve them from violation (i.e. textual corruption, piracy etc.).

Thus the Aldermanbury monument is a duplication of the literary monument that is the First Folio. Since it honours Heminge and Condell rather than Shakespeare, it appears to commemorate the editorial construct rather than the eternally living author; in its lapidary form it memorializes the book above the lives of those who contributed to its publication. What the world owes to Heminge and Condell is not

'Shakespeare', but 'all that it calls Shakespeare', a culturally constructed artefact that inevitably seems detached from the originating author. But this detachment had already of course been effected in the paratextual matter of the First Folio itself, where Shakespeare the author is clearly absented from the scene of production, and the plays ritually called together in order to construct a new author-function that replaces the dead author. The monument completes this process of uncoupling Shakespeare the author from Shakespeare the man.

Hence this literary monument to the First Folio belongs in the garden which was a churchyard, where it commemorates the buried editors who worshipped at the vanished mediaeval church. Or to put it another way, the Aldermanbury monument is a petrified duplication of the bibliographical monument that is the Folio. But does it have any but a coincidental connection with the subsequently acquired significance of the garden as a war memorial? We need first to establish what kind of war memorial this is. The garden remembers the Second World War from a particular perspective, one that is quite different, as the signatories to 'Ruined City Churches' observed, from the ubiquitous cenotaphs that remembered the fallen of the First World War. The latter list primarily the names of those killed in action, and are imbrued with the heroic and elegiac culture we see re-enacted on each annual Remembrance Day, encapsulated in the continuing use in inscriptions and church liturgies of Laurence Binyon's 'For the Fallen'.[34] The Aldermanbury garden remembers the war on the Home Front, 'the Blitz', the war of Hitler's strategic bombing campaign that devastated London and other British cities in 1940–1941. St Mary's was struck by an incendiary bomb on the night of 30 December 1940. This is how *The Times* reported the devastation begun on the 29 December, when St Paul's was hit:[35]

Fire Bombs Rained On London

Waves of enemy aircraft attacked London for some hours last night, raining hundreds of incendiary bombs indiscriminately over a wide area of the capital and its outskirts. The enemy appeared to be concentrating on setting fire to as many buildings as possible.

The next night, 30 December, St Mary's was one of eight Wren churches damaged or destroyed.[36] Noel Mander, a soldier on leave, watched St Mary's collapse:

> I saw that night St Mary, Aldermanbury; St Vedast-alias-Foster, my own church – I saw them all burn, and it was a sensation that I will never forget – hearing the bells fall down the tower, hearing the organ burn, because the hot air blowing through the organ pipes almost sounded as if the poor old organs were shrieking in agony at their destruction.[37]

The emphasis in the press reports is on the cruelty of the attacks, the intensity of the suffering inflicted, the heroism of firefighters and other Home Front defenders, and the refusal of the British people to accept defeat. As Prime Minister Churchill inspected the ruins on the following day, according to *The Times*, people sang snatches of the old First World War song 'Tipperary': 'Are we downhearted? No!' This music-hall insouciance of the blitzed population has been questioned, condemned as mere propaganda, and even ridiculed.[38] But though the public emotion may not have been as 'resolutely cheerful' as *The Times* insisted, it was certainly one of heroic endurance and stubborn determination. Churchill's speech of September 1940, cited in the same *Times* article, genuinely captured and set the tone of the nation:[39]

> These cruel, wanton, indiscriminate bombings of London are, of course, a part of Hitler's invasion plan. He hopes, by killing large numbers of civilians, and women and children that he will terrorize and cow the people of this Mighty Imperial city [...]. Little does he know the spirit of the British nation, or the tough fibre of the Londoners whose forebears played a leading part in the establishment of Parliamentary institutions and who have been bred to value freedom far above their lives [...]. What he has done is to kindle a fire in British hearts, here and all over the world, which will glow long after all traces of the conflagrations he has caused in London have been removed. He has lighted a fire which will burn with a steady and consuming flame until the last vestiges of Nazi tyranny have been burnt out of Europe, and until the Old World and the New can join hands to rebuild the temples of man's freedom and man's honour on foundations which will not soon or easily be overthrown.

Churchill went on to pay tribute to the men and women working for the nation's defences, air-raid wardens and firefighters, those whose exemplary fortitude and courage constituted a form of domestic heroism:

> I express my admiration for the exemplary manner in which all the air-raid precaution services in London are being discharged, especially the fire brigades, whose work has been so heavy and also dangerous.

These were the unsung heroes celebrated by T.S. Eliot, Kensington air-raid warden, in his 'Defence of the Islands': those 'for whom the paths of glory are / The lanes and the streets of Britain'.[40] The British people, Churchill says, are 'a people who will not flinch or weary of the struggle, hard and protracted though it will be', but will 'rather draw from the heart of suffering itself the means of inspiration and survival, and of a victory won not only for ourselves, but for all – a victory won not only for our own times, but for the long and better days that are to come'.

As a war memorial, the Aldermanbury garden does not commemorate the heroism and sacrifice of the front line, as did the cenotaphs of the First World War. In this war, wrote the signatories of the 12 August 1944 letter to *The Times*, 'conditions have been different. England itself has been in the battle and London is still in it'. The garden remembers not those warriors who fell on far-off battlefields, but rather the little people, the men, women, and children, the young and old and unborn, who endured the war on the Home Front. Those who, night after 'interminable night',[41] suffered violence from the air, and day after day crawled out of the shelters or the ruins to begin life all over again; or were taken out dead from the rubble; or were never seen again, and remained to rest in unvisited tombs. And here we can identify the deeper congruence that links the meaning of the gardens, and the meaning of the statue that was erected some seventy years before the Blitz, and almost exactly a century before the church's westward migration. For through the Aldermanbury monument, Heminge and Condell are commemorated precisely as such heroes of the people, ordinary men whose virtuous actions secured for them an extraordinary destiny. They were only ancillary participants in the gestation of the theatrical work that became the Folio, but without their disinterested and charitable intervention, there would have been no Folio: nothing for the world to call Shakespeare. In the same way the victims of the Blitz were passive sufferers, on the receiving end of military action, and yet essential contributors to the ultimate victory over fascism.

In his treatise Charles Clement Walker provides a brief biographical sketch of Shakespeare, following the narrative of Rowe's biography. He clearly had no problem accepting Shakespeare's humble origins as the son of a tradesman, possibly a butcher, and his lack of formal education. As a philanthropic Victorian industrialist Walker was only too happy to think of Shakespeare emerging from such an underprivileged background, and bearing with him to London a promising package of Victorian values. Shakespeare had both ability and 'industry', but also virtues of temperance and steadiness that rendered him a more reliable asset to the theatre than the typically dissolute university men who wrote for it. Shakespeare, says Walker, probably began to make his way as a writer since he was always there to patch up scripts while the wits were recovering from their debaucheries. As a craftsman, actor, and writer, Shakespeare was concerned only with professional success, and cared nothing about the preservation of his work. If the survival of the works had depended on him, then all would have been lost, either through careless dispersion, or in some such disaster as the burning of the Globe:

> There could hardly be anything more hopeless when the earth closed on Shakespeare's grave than the expectation that any more would be heard of his unprinted plays, beyond the applause that they might be greeted with when produced at the Globe Theatre, whose property almost, if not entirely they were; for there were numerous other dramas which were played to suit the public taste for novelty and change, and there is no evidence that his plays would have had any other fate than those dramas, of which most have passed away, forgotten or perished.[42]

Fortunately for posterity, however, the works were rescued from the flames and preserved by men who were neither dissolute university wits, nor insouciant bohemian artists, but solid and public-spirited citizens.[43] The works were salvaged from that moral and literal conflagration, conveyed across the river, securely deposited inside the City, and used to prepare the First Folio for publication. Heminge and Condell displayed themselves through this undertaking to be honest and ingenuous men, modest and unassuming in their approach, industrious and careful in their procedures. Their motivation was purely charitable, since they looked for no profit from the undertaking, and undertook the work purely out of friendship, concern for the public interest, and respect for the memory of their late friend and colleague.

Although the monument was erected to remember Heminge and Condell, and their indispensible contribution to the preservation of 'all that we call Shakespeare', their lives are relatively anonymized rather than foregrounded. No attempt was made to represent them, since there are no surviving physical likenesses to reproduce, and it is Shakespeare's effigy that commands the structure. Although the monument was designed to install Heminge and Condell into the public memory, they are paradoxically huddled back under Shakespeare's shadow. All three men are in another sense absorbed into the monument that is the book; but the book remains synonymous in the public mind with the name 'Shakespeare'. In commemorating Heminge and Condell, Walker was trying to do what Thomas Hardy attempted at around the same time in *Jude the Obscure* (1895) for 'the struggling men and women' of the working class, those who were 'the reality of Christminster, though they knew little of Christ or Minster'. In this 'palpitating, varied, and compendious [...] book of humanity' that is the common people, Jude recognizes himself:

> He saw that his destiny lay not with these, but among the manual toilers in the shabby purlieu which he himself occupied, unrecognized as part of the city at all by its visitors and panegyrists, yet without whose denizens the hard readers could not read nor the high thinkers live.[44]

In the end it is of course the name of Christminster that is remembered, but Hardy at least sought to reveal some of its hidden histories. As a war memorial, Aldermanbury Gardens remembers the past in a similar way, from the perspective of the disappeared. History is written here not from the vantage point of the victors, but on behalf of the defeated, the vanished who were buried under the rubble, many of whom share with Heminge and Condell the communal graveyard of blitzed London.[45] Their bodies were dispersed and scattered, their names lost and forgotten. But they are there, buried 'deep with the first dead', to be mourned and 're-membered' in this quiet and unassuming spot.[46] Their traces remain in the air, fittingly housed by the memory of the church that is also gone, but not forgotten.

Jennifer Wallace wrote of another 'blitz', 11 September 2001, as an event that challenged the capacities of memory. She describes two 'public projects for retrieving and mourning the dead' from the World Trade Centre:[47]

> One was the grim excavation of the rubble at Ground Zero and the search for traces of the 2,823 people who died there. The other was the daily publication in the *New York Times* of a brief biography of each victim, a 200–word profile accompanied by a photograph which soon became well known collectively as the 'Portraits of Grief'.

The portraits are themselves 'powerful works of tragedy bringing a human dimension to an inhuman disaster', and 'giving shape to the disaster by transforming ordinary lives into significant narratives'. Wallace then compares the search for traces of the 2,823 people who died with examples from classical tragedy: the literal and figurative disintegration of the body, and the human effort to reassemble or reconstruct, to re-member what has been dispersed and fragmented, to be found in *The Bacchae* and *Hamlet*. The archaeological excavation of Ground Zero was a search for certainty in the recovery of remains, a work of mourning like Agave's desire to have the limbs of her dismembered son 'joined decently together'; or like Hamlet's mission to 'set [...] right' a disjointed time.

As the excavation progressed, it became increasingly obvious that nowhere near all the victims would be accounted for. Wallace quotes a firefighter, faced with a dwindling pile of rubble and a list of 1,800 people still untraced: 'You've got a great number of people that you want to find, and you've got a certain amount of dirt that's left. And there's a gap. That gap is going to be a sorrowful one'. The 'gap' is literally, as Wallace observes, between 'statistics and physical dust'. But as a 'gap' of sorrow, it also represents the space of tragedy, the lacuna between hope and despair, between 'consolation and disillusion'. Such gaps are the enduring legacy of unnatural disasters like the Blitz, or 9/11, or the 7 July bombings in London. But gaps to be bridged, as Wallace observes, holes to be filled with memory and mourning, spaces in which to 'write stories.'

Aldermanbury gardens is also one of history's holes, a gap from which life and matter have been evacuated, leaving an empty space free for the exercising of memory. The Aldermanbury monument remembers Shakespeare not as a great individual genius, but as a pluralistic body consisting of many members. 'For the body', as St

Paul observed, 'is not one member, but many' (1 Corinthians 12.14). Prominent among the associated members who are part of the body of Shakespeare are Heminge and Condell. Here, in this garden, they are appropriately remembered, their reputations fittingly restored, for as Paul says, 'those *members* of the body, which we think to be less honourable, upon these we bestow more abundant honour' (1 Corinthians 12.23). The monument invites a Eucharistic commemoration, in which every member is a part of the whole: 'though we are many, we are one body'. On the site of the old church, the elusive traces of those *disjecta membra* that were our forebears are also brought together in the same kind of loving remembrance, 'folded in a single party'.[48]

This double function of memory as reconstruction and recuperation is firmly embedded inside the First Folio. One of the commendatory poems affixed to the 1632 Folio edition of *Mr William Shakespeare's Comedies, Histories and Tragedies*, under the superscription 'I.M.S.' depicts the dramatist's mind as a mirror that can bring an image of the past into immediate visibility:[49]

> A mind reflecting ages past, whose clear
> And equal surface can make things appear
> Distant a thousand years, and represent
> Them in their lively colours' just extent ... (ll. 1–4).

The mirror of Shakespeare's mind makes available, to present vision, images of a remote past, causes things that are 'distant a thousand years' to *appear*. But it also simulates a past reality by using a contemporary performative medium, makes present things *appear to be* distant a thousand years. To represent, and to re-present; to familiarize and to estrange. Shakespeare's imagination could make things from a thousand years ago *appear*, but he could do so only by making his stage and his actors take on the convincing *appearance* of a thousand-year-old reality.

The poem thus grasps the two-way process of commemoration, in which the past has to be made to be re-made, its reconstruction being also its initial construction. At the same time the 'things' recollected from the past clearly retain their own integrity, or there would be no sense in which they could be misrepresented. The past was alive, is now dead, but can be revived by the power of memory.

We do not simply make up the past as we go along. But where is it? Confronted with the elegist's question, *ubi sunt?*, we can only reply, *Hic et ubique*. Here, there, and everywhere. Not a trace remains on this spot of Wren's church of St Mary Aldermanbury. Yet the garden remembers it.

> Old stone to new building, old timber to new fires,
> Old fires to ashes, and ashes to the earth ...[50]

Of the Blitz the garden formally commemorates, nothing beside remains. But the space is full of memory, and as Evelyn Waugh observed, 'we possess nothing certainly except the past'.[51] Chemical scientists speak of inanimate substances such as water having a 'memory'. Experiments show that 'much diluted solutions appear to behave as though they contain absent solutes that had once been present'.[52] These observations seem to confute the fact that the hydrogen bonds holding molecules of water together break so easily and rapidly. Yet as Martin Chaplin indicates, 'the behaviour of a large population of water molecules may be retained even if that of individual molecules is constantly changing. Such behaviour is easy to observe: a sea wave may cross an ocean, remaining a wave and with dependence on its history, but its molecular content is continuously changing'.[53] A church like St Mary's, observed Hugh Casson, stands, 'even when in ruins, upon sacred ground'. The sanctity conferred by the consecration of a building somehow survives that building's destruction.[54] But whence does such 'sacredness' derive? What the memory of the ruined church remembers is not merely an ecclesiastical ritual, but the suffering of a people. The churches have, in Casson's words, 'undergone the physical trials of war, and bear its scars'. This is the place's memory, and it is in this sense that 'every stone and fragment of the past is part of the pattern of history'.[55]

Walker presented Heminge and Condell as emblems of self-sacrifice, businessmen who yet undertook their work 'without the hope of profit', motivated by 'disinterested affection', unselfish love and 'unaffected modesty'.[56] The memory of the Blitz also recalls sacrifice, and the use of a commemorative monument would be 'to remind posterity of the reality of the sacrifices upon which its apparent security has been built'.[57] The British people, Churchill affirmed, would never admit defeat, but would 'rather draw from the heart of suffering itself the means of inspiration and survival'. The loss of individual prestige or personal fame entailed in publishing a great writer's book, or in assisting anonymously in a great humanitarian war effort, represent parallel forms of the self-sacrifice theologically defined as *kenosis*, the voluntary emptying of the self into a greater purpose.

In Dante's *Purgatorio* the spirit of Arnaut Daniel begs Dante to remember him, and pray for him, in order to help assuage his suffering, '*Tempra ma dolour*'. Then he turns to embrace the purgatorial flame, and is lost in the refining fire: '*Poi s'ascose nel foco che gli affina*'.

The story of Aldermanbury Gardens is a story of fire. Beginning with the destruction of the mediaeval church of St Mary the Virgin in the Great Fire of London, to the conflagration that ruined Wren's church in 1940, the site has endured ordeal after ordeal, 'consumed by either fire or fire'.[58] Wren's church was a phoenix that twice rose from the ashes, unfurled its wings, and flew away westwards. The First Folio commemorated by the Aldermanbury monument was perhaps, if Shakespeare's manuscripts did (as some have thought) perish in the fire that destroyed the Globe theatre, another phoenix resurrection, keeping alive the eternal flame of Shakespeare's genius. 'Age has not dimmed its brightness', wrote Charles Clement Walker. The garden remembers the incendiary violence of war, but also that fire of patriotic pride identified (convincingly at that point in history) by Churchill with the great cause of humanity:

> What [Hitler] has done is to kindle a fire in British hearts, here and all over the world, which will glow long after all traces of the conflagrations he has caused in London have been removed. He has lighted a fire which will burn with a steady and consuming flame until the last vestiges of Nazi tyranny have been burnt out of Europe, and until the Old World and the New can join hands to rebuild the temples of man's freedom and man's honour on foundations which will not soon or easily be overthrown.

Churchill's rhetoric echoes Foxe's *Book of Martyrs*, and the words Latimer is said to have spoken to Ridley before he was enveloped by the flames: 'Be of good cheer, Ridley; and play the man. We shall this day, by God's grace, light up such a candle in England, as I trust, will never be put out'. Thus the pyrotechnic devastation of London is redefined as creative sacrifice by reference back to the 'intolerable shirt of flame' worn by the Protestant martyrs.[59]

Amidst the ruins of London's churches, in the aftermath of the Blitz, Hugh Casson saw the efflorescence of new vegetable growth replacing, but also replicating, the fires that had recently devoured them: 'among the shabby heaps of stones, flowering with willow-herb as pink and lively as the flames which earlier sprouted from their crevices'. Air-raid warden T.S. Eliot saw the same persistent synthesis of suffering and creativity, the same ubiquitous merging of flower with flame:

> When the tongues of flame are in-folded
> Into the crowned knot of fire
> And the fire and the rose are one.[60]

Like the church at Little Gidding, Aldermanbury Garden is another place where it is possible to find 'the intersection of the timeless moment'; England and nowhere; never and always.[61] A place where silent voices can be heard. A place where the dead can, at last, have their say.

> And what the dead had no speech for, when living,
> They can tell you, being dead: the communication
> Of the dead is tongued with fire beyond the language of the living.[62]

Graham Holderness is the author or editor of some 60 books. His work can be divided into three strands: literary criticism, theory and scholarship, especially in Shakespeare studies; the pioneering of an innovative new method of 'creative criticism'; and creative writing in fiction, poetry and drama. Key critical works include *The Shakespeare Myth* (Manchester UP, 1988), *The Politics of Theatre and Drama* (Routledge, 1992), *Shakespeare: The Histories* (Bloomsbury, 2000), and *The Faith of William Shakespeare* (Lion Books, 2016). Works of creative criticism, which are half criticism and half fiction, include *Nine Lives of William Shakespeare* (Bloomsbury-Arden Shakespeare, 2011); *Tales from Shakespeare: Creative Collisions* (Cambridge University Press, 2014) and *Re-writing Jesus: Christ in 20th Century Fiction and Film* (Bloomsbury, November 2014). He has also published two novels: *The Prince of Denmark* (University of Hertfordshire Press, 2001), and the historical fantasy novel *Black and Deep Desires: William Shakespeare Vampire Hunter* (Top Hat Books, 2015).

Notes

1. This empirical study builds on previous critical and theoretical work I have undertaken concerning history, memory, and mourning. See especially *Shakespeare: The Histories* (London: Macmillan, 2000); *Textual Shakespeare: Writing and the Word* (Hatfield: University of Hertfordshire Press, 2003); 'Vanishing Point: Looking for *Hamlet*', *Shakespeare* 1:2 (December 2005), 154–73; '"Mots d'escalier": Clio, Orpheus, Eurydice', in *Shakespeare's Histories and Counter-Histories*, ed. Stuart Hampton-Reeves, Dermot Cavanagh, and Steve Longstaffe (Manchester: Manchester University Press, 2006), 219–40; and '"I covet your skull": Desire and Death in *Hamlet*', *Shakespeare Survey* 60 (2007), 223–36. I have left implicit the obvious parallels, especially in terms of reconstruction debates, between the Blitz of 1940 and 9/11; but for the latter see my 'Shakespeare and Terror', in *Shakespeare Yearbook: Shakespeare after 9/11*, ed. Matthew Biberman, Julia Reinhardt Lupton, and Graham Holderness (Lewiston, Queenston, and Lampeter: The Edwin Mellen Press, 2010). I am grateful to my wife Marilyn Holderness for finding Aldermanbury gardens, and for help with 'the memory of water'.
2. A garden in the city.
3. It has of course been argued that they did not act as editors. See John Dover Wilson, 'The Task of Heminge and Condell', in *Studies in the First Folio* (London: Oxford University Press, 1924), 54–55. Doubt has also been cast on their authorship of the dedication and address 'To the Great Variety of Readers'. The monument is a tribute to practical men, commemorating what they did, rather than what they said, and my arguments do not depend on any assumptions about their literary or scholarly capacities.
4. Philip Ward Jackson describes the bust as 'a painstaking attempt to amalgamate the two portraits of Shakespeare which were supposed to possess a flawless pedigree'. See *Public Sculpture of the City of London* (Liverpool: Liverpool University Press, 2003), 2.
5. 'To the Most Noble and Incomparable Paire of Brethren', in *Mr. William Shakespeare's Comedies, Histories & Tragedies: A Facsimile of the First Folio 1623* (London: Routledge, 1998).
6. Heminge and Condell both served as 'sidesmen' in the church. Charles Connell in *They Gave Us Shakespeare: John Heminge and Henry Condell* (Stocksfield: Oriel Press, 1982) incorrectly describes them as 'churchwardens'. In the Anglican church sidespeople report to churchwardens.
7. The same qualifying assertion is to be found in Connell's *They Gave Us Shakespeare*, which begins with a survey of the Aldermanbury monument, and recuperates Walker's tone and line of argument: 'without their devotion, assiduity and indefatigable efforts, the world would have been poorer by what is generally referred to as the Shakespeare canon' (2). See also Christian E. Hauer, Jr., and William A. Young, *A Comprehensive History of the London Church and Parish of St Mary, the Virgin, Aldermanbury: The Phoenix of Aldermanbury* (Lewiston: Edwin Mellen Press, 1994): 'their contribution to the preservation of his works cannot be overestimated' (80).
8. Laurie E. Maguire, 'Composition/Decomposition: Singular Shakespeare and the Death of the Author', in *The Renaissance Text: Theory, Editing, Textuality*, ed. Andrew Murphy (Manchester: Manchester University Press, 2000), 135–53 (p. 139).

9. Jackson, *Public Sculpture*, 2.
10. Charles Clement Walker, *John Heminge and Henry Condell, Friends and Fellow-actors of Shakespeare, and What the World Owes to Them* (London: privately printed, 1896).
11. Walker, *John Heminge and Henry Condell*, 3.
12. Walker, *John Heminge and Henry Condell*, 4.
13. Henry Irving placed the same emphasis in the speech he delivered at the unveiling. In October of the same year, laying the foundation stone of the Dulwich Public Library, Irving had eulogized Edward Alleyn as a fellow 'player'; and in his speech at the unveiling in Aldermanbury of a monument to Heminge and Condell, he had taken the same tone: 'these two players who lived in affectionate friendship to another player, William Shakespeare'. Austin Brereton, *The Life of Henry Irving* (London: Longman, Green, 1908), 2:254.
14. Walker, *John Heminge and Henry Condell*, 6.
15. Walker, *John Heminge and Henry Condell*, 5–6.
16. An example is the red granite obelisk in the grounds of St Philip's Cathedral in Birmingham.
17. Eric de Mare, *Wren's London* (London: Folio Society, 1975), 87.
18. Quoted in Peter J. Larkham and Joe Nasr, 'Bombed Churches as Memorials and Mementoes: Physical Traces in the Urban Landscape', 12–13. Available at www.lhds.bcu.ac.uk/.../Birmingham_churches_conference_paper_spoken_2.doc [Accessed 2 February 2010].
19. Quoted Larkham and Nasr, 'Bombed Churches', 6.
20. *The Times*, 15 August 1944.
21. *Bombed Churches as War Memorials* (Cheam: Architectural Press, 1945). A reprint of the August 1944 letter to *The Times* forms the frontispiece.
22. *Bombed Churches as War Memorials*, 21.
23. Cf. T.S. Eliot: 'Water and fire shall rot / The marred foundations we forgot / Of sanctuary and choir'. 'Little Gidding', *Collected Poems* (London: Faber and Faber, 1963), 216.
24. *Bombed Churches as War Memorials*, 11–12.
25. Hauer and Young, *Phoenix of Aldermanbury*, 359.
26. The Doha Players Theatre, destroyed by a suicide-bomber, is planned to re-appear as the 'Phoenix Theatre' of Qatar. See Graham Holderness and Bryan Loughrey, '"Rudely Interrupted": Shakespeare and Terrorism', *Critical Survey* 19:3 (2007), 107–23.
27. A management consultancy company offering 'strategic counsel' and investment advice goes by the name of 'Heminge and Condell', though the names of the partners are Wilkinson and Eidinow. The company name invokes the historic Heminge and Condell partnership as a model of constructive facilitation.
28. 'It may be noted that this is the only public bust of Shakespeare in the City of London' (Walker, *John Heminge and Henry Condell*, 26). One of the residential blocks in the Barbican is called 'Shakespeare Tower' (see my *Shakespeare Myth* [Manchester: Manchester University Press, 1988], 'Introduction').
29. The illustration in Walker's pamphlet (facing p. 25) enhances this effect by showing the Folio enlarged and re-scaled relative to the monument.
30. John Weever, *Ancient Funeral Monuments* (London, 1631), B1r.

31. Maguire, 'Composition/Decomposition', 142.
32. Maguire, 139.
33. Maguire, 138.
34. Walker's phrase 'Age has not dimmed its brightness' echoes Shakespeare's Cleopatra ('Age cannot wither her') and anticipates Binyon's now famous 'Age shall not weary them' from 'For the Fallen'.
35. *The Times*, 30 December 1940, p. 1
36. Hauer and Young state that the church was hit on 29 December, but the *Times* reports appear to indicate that it was on the following night. *Phoenix of Aldermanbury*, 353.
37. Quoted in Hauer and Young, *Phoenix of Aldermanbury*, 354–55.
38. Especially in Angus Calder's *The Myth of the Blitz* (London: Jonathan Cape, 1990).
39. Quoted in *The Times*, 12 September 1940, p. 1.
40. 'Defence of the Islands', *Collected Poems*.
41. T.S. Eliot, 'Little Gidding', *Collected Poems*, 220.
42. Walker, *John Heminge and Henry Condell*, 13.
43. A grocer and a publican, as they are sometimes scathingly described.
44. Thomas Hardy, *Jude the Obscure* (London: Penguin, 1995), 118.
45. 'Ruined City Churches' calls for 'a memorial to the thousands of Londoners who died in the Blitz for whom those walls of calcined stone were once not monuments, but tombs'.
46. Dylan Thomas, 'A Refusal to Mourn the Death by Fire of a Child in London', *Deaths and Entrances* (London: J. M. Dent, 1946), 8.
47. Jennifer Wallace, 'Tragedy grapples with gap between human meaningfulness and despair', *Times Higher Education Supplement*, 6 September 2002, p. 16. Later expanded as '"We Can't Make More Dirt ...": Tragedy and the Excavated Body', *Cambridge Quarterly* 32:2 (2003), 103–11.
48. Eliot, 'Little Gidding', *Collected Poems*, 220.
49. 'I.M.S.', 'On Worthy Master Shakespeare and his Poems' (1632), in *William Shakespeare: The Complete Works*, ed. Stanley Wells and Gary Taylor (Oxford: Oxford University Press, 1987), xli.
50. Eliot, 'East Coker', *Collected Poems*, 196.
51. Evelyn Waugh, *Brideshead Revisited* (London: Penguin, 1945), 203.
52. Martin F. Chaplin, 'The Memory of Water: An Overview', *Homeopathy* 96:3 (July 2007), 143.
53. Martin F. Chaplin, 'The Memory of Water', 144. See also my '"Dressing Old Words New": Shakespeare, Science, and Appropriation', *Borrowers and Lenders: The Journal of Shakespeare and Appropriation* 1:2 (Fall/Winter, 2006).
54. For the difficult relationship between place and the sacred see my 'Rome, Multiversal City: The Material and the Immaterial in Religious Tourism', *Cross Currents* 59:3 (Autumn 2009) (New York: Wiley Blackwell), 342–48; and '"The undiscovered country": Philip Pullman and the "Land of the Dead"', *Literature and Theology* 21:3 (September 2007), 276–92.
55. 'History is a pattern / Of timeless moments'. See 'Little Gidding', *Collected Poems*, 222.
56. Walker, *John Heminge and Henry Condell*, 4.
56. *The Times*, 15 August 1944.
57. Eliot, 'Little Gidding', *Collected Poems*, 221.

59. Eliot, 'Little Gidding', *Collected Poems*, 221.
60. Eliot, 'Little Gidding', *Collected Poems*, 223.
61. Eliot, 'Little Gidding', *Collected Poems*, 215.
62. Eliot, 'Little Gidding', *Collected Poems*, 215.

Chapter 5
American Shakespeare Clubs and Commemoration

Katherine Scheil

At the turn of the twentieth century, over 500 Shakespeare clubs, comprising mainly women, met across America, in small rural towns and large cities alike. Most clubs met every other week to read, study, and perform Shakespeare, from Selma, Alabama to Eugene, Oregon. As well as their own self-improvement, most Shakespeare clubs took an active role in civic and community life and engaged in a number of initiatives designed to improve the cultural, social, and intellectual climate of their communities. They were also involved with forms of commemoration – both with memorializing Shakespeare and with creating a history of their own intellectual efforts. The history of the Portia Club of Avon, Illinois commemorates typical clubwomen

> who studied, memorized and acted in Shakespeare's plays, learned about the continents of the world [...] cooked dinners, held bake sales, sold fruitcakes, pushed for better education, helped with food for school children, supported Federation charities, proved women were smart enough to vote [...] attended meetings regardless of weather, believed that an educated mother was a better mother, were devoted to their community, wanted to bring new ideas from all over the world, wrote essays by hand and by lamplight.[1]

Notes for this section begin on page 75.

These women were not just reading Shakespeare; they were carrying out a serious program of civic engagement and self-education underneath a veneer of domestic improvement, sanctioned by Shakespeare, which they preserved for posterity in a variety of ways. In this essay, I am concerned with the ways in which Shakespeare clubs in America wove Shakespeare into what Susan Bennett calls the 'social fabric of remembering', through public projects, private rituals, and the transformation of domestic practices into commemorative acts.[2] Though largely forgotten in the history of Shakespeare in America, these hundreds of clubs can help explain Shakespeare's pervasiveness in American culture.

Public Commemorations

Numerous Shakespeare clubs combined their goals of improving their minds and enhancing their communities, while at the same time commemorating Shakespeare as a symbol of progress, improvement, and community betterment. Most clubs took part in social outreach projects, which linked Shakespeare's cultural value with intellectual development and civic responsibility; one 1880 account even described women's clubs as 'the popular custodians of literature in America'.[3] Many of their public commemorations still survive and continue to preserve Shakespeare in the physical landscape of local communities.

When they were not reading Shakespeare, most clubs were involved in a combination of local and international causes, which created a history of Shakespeare-sponsored public activism. The Shakespeare Round Table Club of Bowling Green, Ohio knitted for soldiers in the First World War and supported a French orphan.[4] Likewise, the Friday Shakespeare Club of Santa Cruz, California knitted and sewed for the Red Cross during both world wars and donated books to the Shakespeare collection at the local library.[5] In addition to celebrating Shakespeare's birthday every year, the Waxahachie, Texas Shakespeare Club started an 'Empty Stocking Crusade' to deliver gifts to needy children at Christmas, a 'Christmas Cheer' project to gather packages for children of workers at nearby cotton mills, furnished a room in the local sanatorium, and worked for the Red Cross during the Second World War.[6] Although few tangible remnants of these projects survive, they nevertheless established the connection between Shakespeare and public service in communities nationwide.

Locally, copious public spaces across America are a result of the commemorative efforts of Shakespeare clubs. A 1927 newspaper article on Shakespeare celebratory gardens described them as a 'worthy enterprise that has proved effective in increasing affection for the great plays, bringing them close to the young folk and reawakening interest of matured readers'.[7] Promoting their Shakespeare Garden, the Shakespeare Class of Toledo (Ohio) leader Mrs. Robert C. Morris remarked that it is 'a healthful thing for the young of the city to see perpetuated the memory of the truly great in an age when false heroes are so greatly worshipped'.[8] Across the country, Shakespeare clubs set up gardens in memory of Shakespeare like the one in Oklahoma City, where the Shakespeare Club sponsored a garden in one of the city's parks, with a bust of Shakespeare and a public celebration of Shakespeare's birthday every April.[9] In Detroit, the Shakespeare Study Club planned a similar Shakespeare garden with a bust of Shakespeare and quotations from the plays. The Woodland Shakespeare Club of California planted trees in a city park and donated a stone bench in memory of Shakespeare. When the Woodland City Hall was built in 1936, a copy of the Shakespeare Club yearbook was placed in one of the building's cornerstones, symbolic of 'the continuing influence of the Club in the community', commemorating both Shakespeare and women's intellectual work.[10]

Several Shakespeare clubs tried to make their memorials authentically 'Shakespearian'. In New Rochelle, New York, the Avon Bard Club maintained a Shakespeare Garden in a local park, 'featuring a sun dial inscribed with a quotation from *The Merchant of Venice* and a luxuriant bed of English ivy, grown from cuttings brought directly from Stratford-upon-Avon'. Likewise, in Plainfield, New Jersey, the Shakespeare club began a Shakespeare garden in 1928 with flowers and shrubs labelled from the plays, making it 'educational, and on many days ladies and teachers with children are found in the garden'. The Cleveland Shakespeare Club sponsored a Shakespeare Garden replete with 'trees from the original Birnam Wood. That Birnam forest should come to Dunsinane seemed to Macbeth impossible, but that saplings from the famous grove should be growing near Lake Erie seems incredible'. The garden also contained 'a luxuriant growth of ivy transplanted from the alleged tomb of Juliet'.[11]

Many Shakespeare clubs memorialized Shakespeare by establishing his works in the American educational system. The Shakespeare Club of Lawton, Oklahoma endowed a scholarship at Cameron University in Lawton for students who plan to teach English in high school.[12] The Waxahachie, Texas Shakespeare club sponsored a $1,000 scholarship at Trinity University and also presented dictionaries to students every year at local schools, sponsored by the husband of a past club president in her memory.[13] In South Dakota, the Aberdeen Shakespeare Club collected funds for a scholarship for a girl to study in Oxford.[14] The philanthropist Mrs. Esther Hermann, a member of the Fortnightly Shakespeare Club of New York City, immortalized her enthusiasm for Shakespeare by donating 'handsome copies of Shakespeare's work as prizes to schools and scholars, or as presents to club libraries'.[15] For scores of club women, meeting to read and discuss Shakespeare also involved improving the world around them, which often resulted in public memorials to Shakespeare.

As a more permanent commemoration of their investment in learning, social progress, and Shakespeare, many clubs took an active role in founding libraries across America, as part of what Michael Rowlands calls 'the material culture of remembering'.[16] Club members raised money for library buildings, helped acquire Carnegie funding for libraries, donated books from their own collections, and often served as librarians.[17] Their determination to establish community libraries embodied their values of 'remembering the past and embracing the future', channelled through Shakespeare.[18] A few representative examples should illustrate the degree to which clubs permeated the development of libraries across the U.S. In the northeast, the Shakespeare Club of Lyndon, Vermont contributed money to the town library, which was housed in a store, with 3,835 books available three afternoons and two evenings a week.[19] Women from the Shakespeare Club in Queens, New York began with a travelling library and then helped raise money for a permanent library.[20] In Concord, New Hampshire the work of the numerous Shakespeare clubs was commemorated with a permanent Shakespeare Room in the Fowler Public Library.[21] In the Midwest, the Shakespeare Round Table Club of Bowling Green, Ohio held bake sales, socials, teas, and other events to raise money for what was eventually the Bowling Green Public Library, and established a school district library based on their own collection.[22] In Hammond,

Indiana the Shakespeare Club began a public library with only fifty books, housed in the Bloomhoff and Company Millinery Store, later supported by a Carnegie grant for a permanent building.[23] In Illinois, the women of the Mt. Vernon Shakespeare Club opened a circulating library in a local department store in 1895, and in 1899 offered to the city 'our books, our bookcases and the use of our club room as a library, free of rent, provided we may select the majority of the directors of the Public Library'.[24]

On the frontier west, Shakespeare clubwomen were equally industrious in their library initiatives. The women of the Shakespeare Club in rural Hot Springs, South Dakota organized their city library in 1898.[25] In Payette, Idaho, the Shakespeare Club began a library with books from their homes, followed by 'five hundred hand-written postcards [...] sent out by members requesting donations of books'.[26] In the South, the Junior Shakespeare Club of Denton, Texas went door-to-door to collect more than 4,000 books for a public library, and the Flatonia, Texas Shakespeare club began the public library with a book donated by each member.[27] The Barnesville, Georgia Shakespearean Club gave a series of lectures and entertainments to help establish a Shakespeare reference library for 'students of all ages and both sexes' to serve the intellectual needs of the community. The club also wanted to commemorate Shakespeare and learning for the future: 'Mindful of the lack of this great advantage in our own youth we desire to prepare better opportunities for our children'.[28] Libraries not only commemorated Shakespeare, they also served as community-building literate practices; as one writer put it in 1904, 'a library is not merely a storehouse for books; it may be a live force and power in the community'.[29]

One of the most compelling examples of clubwomen's efforts to both preserve Shakespeare publicly and to secure his future cultural value comes from the Dallas Shakespeare Club, whose founder Bobbie Cullum purchased a Shakespeare First Folio to donate to the Dallas Public Library in honour of the club's 100th anniversary in 1986. Cullum had the Folio restored by the Folger Shakespeare Library staff, and then she paid for a Brink's truck to transport it to Dallas, where it now resides in a special case in the Dallas Public Library, appropriately placed near the broadside copy of the Declaration of Independence as a permanent memorial to Shakespeare and to the women who found inspiration in his works.[30]

Private Commemorations

The process by which clubs memorialized Shakespeare was extensive, as I have already suggested – in public libraries, monuments, gardens, scholarships, and other civic projects that prevented Shakespeare from becoming forgotten. A more subtle way that clubs kept the memory of Shakespeare alive was through the private practice of memorization. Club members were often required to memorize passages from Shakespeare in the privacy of their homes, and then recite them at roll call. For example, the women of The Sisters' Shakespeare Society of Elizabeth, New Jersey had to 'memorize and give a quotation from some play at each meeting'.[31] The sixty-four women in the Shakespeariana Club of Grand Rapids, Michigan were encouraged to 'commit to memory the most note-worthy thoughts contained in the play' as part of their reading, and they began their celebration of Shakespeare's birthday in 1888 with all sixty members reciting 'Shakespearian mottoes suitable to the occasion'.[32] The Round Table Club of Quincy, Illinois began each meeting with 'Class quotations', and the Avon Club of Concord, New Hampshire 'exercised' their memory by reciting quotations, which they collected in a colloquy for Shakespeare's birthday, 'deemed worthy of being loaned to a club in another city, to be used at a similar gathering'.[33] Meetings of the Woodland, California Shakespeare Club illustrate how memorization worked to preserve Shakespeare: 'Discussion went on freely. Often a member might be reminded of a similar passage in another play and would quote from memory'.[34]

The process of memorizing lines from Shakespeare is perhaps more important than it might seem at first. In *Metaphors of Memory: A History of Ideas About the Mind*, Douwe Draaisma remarks that 'Remembering is precisely reliving something, plus the consciousness that the experience can be located in one's personal past'.[35] For the individual readers who memorized Shakespeare, this process had additional significance. As Louis B. Wright comments, 'Memorizing and reciting the jewels of Shakespeare became an evidence of culture [in America]. This manifestation was not academically inspired but developed directly from folk interest'.[36] Memorizing Shakespeare was a subtle but pervasive way of upholding Shakespeare as a vibrant part of cultural knowledge, and keeping Shakespeare's works 'active and alive, as opposed to mere objects of collection'.[37]

Domestic Commemorations

One of the intriguing aspects of many Shakespeare clubs is their use of domestic practices such as cooking and scrapbooking as a way to commemorate Shakespeare and celebrate their own intellectual work. Many women integrated Shakespeare into their household labour, through such activities as cooking and baking for their Shakespeare club, compiling elaborate programmes for club meetings, planning banquets and Shakespeare's birthday celebrations, and making detailed scrapbooks of club history and activities. The Avon Club of Topeka, Kansas, for example, hosted an annual 'banquet in honor of their Patron Saint' around Shakespeare's birthday, as did most clubs across the country.[38] The San Antonio Shakespeare Club had an annual banquet, where a 'white marble bust of Shakespeare that is a fixture of the Shakespeare Club meetings was draped in pink roses for the organization's Twelfth Night Revel' at the home of club members.[39] The Woodland, California Shakespeare Club held an annual birthday picnic with a trademark cake made by the same member for twenty years, often inviting other California clubs to come; in 1904 the picnic encompassed over 150 clubwomen.[40] The Peoria Women's Club more formally combined food and performance of Shakespeare, with an annual 'Shakespeare Breakfast' prepared by a committee who served shrimp salad every year.[41] The Shakespeariana Club of Grand Rapids, Michigan had a Shakespeare Chest where they preserved 'a luncheon cloth on which the early members inscribed their names in embroidery'.[42]

While these endeavours might seem inconsequential, the incorporation of domestic practices familiar to women helped create what Kate Flint describes as 'a safe space in which [women] could take the imaginative narratives as a jumping-off point for a discussion of what was happening in their lives, [and in] their country', and also as a way to use gendered household practices to celebrate and remember Shakespeare.[43] One of the more unusual examples of this comes from the Fredonia, New York Shakespeare Club, which celebrated Shakespeare's birthday in 1888 'by an entertainment addressed to both the physical and mental nature'. As part of their banquet, they included a course called an 'intellectual salad', which consisted of 'lettuce leaves made of tissue paper of different tints of green', with a Shakespeare quotation written on each leaf. Members could take leaves as long as they continued to correctly identify the source play. The winners received copies of appropriately chosen books: 'Shakespeare Birthday Book' or 'Shakespeare Forget-me-nots'.[44] These various activities inserted Shakespeare into 'a sphere of activity widely considered to be women's domain – cooking and entertaining', and rewarded those women who could best remember (and thus commemorate) Shakespeare.[45]

One club in particular might serve as a representative case study of the use of domestic practices to commemorate Shakespeare and celebrate women's intellectual work. The Anne Hudgins Shakespeare Class of Marietta, Georgia has been meeting for nearly eighty years, in the homes of members, most of whom are descendents of the founding families of the city of Marietta. The club was initiated by Anne Hudgins as a way of maintaining her intellectual life when she moved from Atlanta to the suburb of Marietta. The current history of the club is kept in the house of one of the founding members of the club, Mary Cole. In her living room is a bust of Shakespeare, along with numerous editions of the plays and works of Shakespeare criticism. Most intriguing is the 'Shakespeare Closet', replete with full runs of the journals *Shakespeare Quarterly* and *Shakespeare Survey*, Shakespeare games, a model of the Globe theatre, and an extensive collection of scrapbooks.

Some of these scrapbooks are related to the Shakespeare Club history, but most of them contain various bits of Shakespeariana, organized alphabetically by play, from *Antony and Cleopatra* to *The Winter's Tale*. The contents include newspaper and magazine clippings about productions, works of Shakespeare criticism, and any items which could be tangentially related to a reference in one of the plays – articles on the epiphany are in the *Twelfth Night* scrapbook, for example. Mary Cole's son remarked that compiling the Shakespeare scrapbook was a task for the entire family on Sundays, where they would sit around the dining room table and paste in the clippings collected by their mother during the week.[46]

According to a recent history of scrapbooking, 'scrapbook and album making was considered a female activity, linked to traditional female concerns of holding families together and preserving nostalgic items'.[47] Shakespeare scrapbooks preserved Shakespeare as an object of nostalgia, but they also diverted domestic labour away from household duties, into the service of Shakespeare. Judy Giles points out that in the fin de siècle, women experienced contradictory domestic identities and were 'sometimes pulled forward as agents of change but at others pushed back as symbolizations of continuity and tradition'.[48] Scrapbooking responded to both initiatives, as a way to preserve continuity and tradition through Shakespeare, but also as a forward-looking way to devote household labour to intellectual work and to commemorate women's accomplishments.[49]

Certainly one of Mary Cole's objectives was to chronicle the history of her own Shakespeare club, in line with goals related to nostalgia and preservation. But we might see additional significance in the fact that Shakespeare is occupying part of the household labour and space, not just for the woman of the house, but for the whole family. Scrapbooking was also a way to produce something from Shakespeare, linking domestic labour to literary culture. As one scholar has described the practice of scrapbooking, 'the reader becomes an author' and the scrapbook takes 'place on the border between reading and authoring'.[50] Through scrapbooking women produced something with and from Shakespeare, which established his place in the home as a product of domestic labour.

These scrapbooks reside in their own designated household space, 'the Shakespeare closet', in the formal dining room, so the product of Shakespeare-centred labour is allocated prime household space. According to one historian, 'as the nineteenth century progressed, the well-to-do dedicated their homes to domesticity, consumption and reproduction rather than to domestic manufacturing or income production', and the home was 'indicative of social and economic standing'.[51] If domestic space can be linked to economic success, the allocation of domestic space to Shakespeare signified his association with economic stability and prosperity.[52] The Cole House in Marietta has additional historical significance – this is not just any closet; according to the Cole family, the previous house on that site was the last house General Sherman burned on way to Atlanta from Kennesaw Mountain. The current house is thus a memorial both to Shakespeare and to a piece of history that is desirable to preserve, again involving nostalgia, production and preservation of an artefact, all within a domestic setting.

Like the carefully preserved club minutes and other artefacts, scrapbooking allowed women to create their own permanent history of reading Shakespeare. The members of the Woman's Shakespeare Club of Flint, Michigan, for example, were asked each week to bring in 'any criticism, or item of information found, which if it were in possible shape was put in a Shakespeare book which was being prepared'.[53] The scrapbook of the Shakespeariana Club of Grand Rapids, Michigan offers further insight into the significance of these domestic practices. Their scrapbook contains club programmes interspersed with clippings from the Stratford, Ontario Shakespeare Festival, reviews of books and articles on Shakespeare, and club photographs. This scrapbook places the club within a larger context of Shakespeare-related activity, as a way to memorialize the significance of these women's activities – they were not just meeting privately to read Shakespeare; they were part of a wider cultural movement involving international theatre, publishing, and scholarship.

We might derive additional meaning from the activities of these clubs – creating scrapbooks, celebrating Shakespeare's birthday, reciting Shakespeare's poetry at meetings, and the like – if we look at them as rituals of commemoration.[54] Paul Connerton argues that 'images of the past and recollected knowledge of the past are conveyed and sustained by (more or less ritual) performances'.[55] Rituals of Shakespeare clubs, like reciting verses at a roll call, memorizing passages, following club protocols, all have lasting effects on members' lives. Connerton remarks that 'whatever is demonstrated in rites permeates also non-ritual behaviour and mentality [...]. Rites have the capacity to give value and meaning to the life of those who perform them'.[56] The Anne Hudgins Shakespeare Class of Marietta, Georgia still engages in just such a practice. For their annual Twelfth Night ceremony, each woman prepares a passage from Shakespeare which summarizes her life in the previous year. After commemorating her year through Shakespeare, she then takes a bough of greenery and throws it into the fireplace, signifying the end of one year and the start of another. Some women have been members of the club for over fifty years, and thus have marked a half century through this Shakespeare-centred ritual.[57]

In his study of memory and American culture, David Thelen asks 'how cultures establish traditions and myths from the past to guide the conduct of their members in the present'.[58] Shakespeare was part of the 'past' that shaped the present for these groups; as Maurice Halbwachs remarks, collective memory 'retains from the past only what still lives or is capable of living in the consciousness of groups keeping the memory alive'.[59] Shakespeare clubs ensured that Shakespeare was not forgotten, through the establishment of public spaces, private rituals, and domestic practices. Shakespeare became ensconced in the home – as material objects (books and busts) and as study material – but he also brought women out of the home through the development of public libraries, gardens, and other projects connected to literacy, education, and civic improvement. In their desire to memorialize Shakespeare, club members simultaneously documented their intellectual history and preserved Shakespeare as a prominent part of American cultural life.

Katherine Scheil is Professor of English at the University of Minnesota. Her publications include *Imagining Shakespeare's Wife: The Afterlife of Anne Hathaway* (Cambridge, 2018), and *She Hath Been Reading: Women and Shakespeare Clubs in America* (Cornell, 2012).

Notes

1. *The History of Portia Club of Avon, Illinois, 1894–1994*.
2. Susan Bennett, *Performing Nostalgia: Shifting Shakespeare and the Contemporary Past* (London and New York: Routledge, 1996), 8. This essay is part of an earlier version of a larger project on Shakespeare clubs in America: *She Hath Been Reading: Women and Shakespeare Clubs in America* (Ithaca, NY: Cornell University Press, 2012).
3. Thomas W. Higginson, 'Women and Men: A Typical Club', *Harper's Bazaar* 22 (30 March 1880), 826–27.
4. 'Shakespeare Round Table of Bowling Green, Ohio', *Shakespeare Quarterly* 7 (1956), 462–63.
5. 'A Brief History of the Friday Shakespeare Club on the Seventy-Fifth Anniversary', MS 104, University Library, University of California, Santa Cruz.
6. Maude Wilson, 'Highlights of 54 Years Listed by City, State Federated Shakespeare Club', newspaper clipping dated 1951, Waxahachie vertical file, Nicholas P. Sims Library, Waxahachie, Texas; 'The Shakespeare Club of Waxahachie, Texas', MS CH TX 003, General Federation of Women's Clubs Archive.
7. *Lewiston [Maine] Daily*, Sunday 19 April 1927, p. 3.
8. 'A Shakespeare Garden for Toledo', *The Shakespeare Association Bulletin* 2:1 (March 1927), 8–9.
9. 'Shakespeare Club of Oklahoma City', *Shakespeare Quarterly* 7 (1956), 462.
10. Esther Bickmore Clark, *The Woodland Shakespeare Club: A History, 1886–1967*. Privately printed. (Woodland, CA, 1968), 21, 23.
11. *The Shakespeare Association Bulletin* 5:4 (October 1930), 186, 188.
12. 'Shakespeare Clubs and Study Groups', *Shakespeare Quarterly* 3 (1952), 394; 'Shakespeare Clubs and Societies', *Shakespeare Quarterly* 7 (1956), 462.
13. Maude Wilson, 'Highlights of 54 Years Listed by City, State Federated Shakespeare Club', newspaper clipping dated 1951, Waxahachie vertical file, Nicholas P. Sims Library, Waxahachie, Texas.
14. Lysbeth Em Benkert, 'Shakespeare on the Prairie: The Shakespeare Club of Aberdeen, South Dakota', in *Borrowers and Lenders: The Journal of Shakespeare and Appropriation* 2 (2006). <http://www.borrowers.uga.edu/cocoon/borrowers/pdf?id=781465>.
15. Margherita Arlina Hamm, 'The Fortnightly Shakespeare Club', *The American Shakespeare Magazine* 3 (1879), 320.

16. 'The Role of Memory in the Transmission of Culture', *World Archaeology* 25:2 (1993), 141–51 (p. 144).
17. See Paula D. Watson, 'Founding Mothers: The Contribution of Women's Organizations to Public Library Development in the United States', *The Library Quarterly* 64:3 (1994), 235, 238.
18. Thomas Augst, 'Introduction' to *Institutions of Reading: The Social Life of Libraries in the United States*, ed. Thomas Augst and Kenneth E. Carpenter (Amherst: University of Massachusetts Press), 4.
19. *Second Biennial Report of the Board of Library Commissioners of Vermont, 1897–98* (St Johnsbury, VT: The Caledonian Company, 1898), 64–65.
20.. <http://www.queenslibrary.org/index.aspx?page_nm=CL-CommunityInfo&branch_id=Q#>.
21. *The History of Concord New Hampshire*, vol. 1, ed. James O. Lyford (Concord: The Rumford Press, 1903), 572, 606. The report of the Stratford Club of Concord in 1959 notes that there were once ten Shakespeare clubs in Concord. *Shakespeare Quarterly* 10:3 (1959), 456.
22. 'Shakespeare Clubs and Societies', *Shakespeare Quarterly* 7 (1956), 462–3. See also <http://wcdpl.lib.oh.us/wcdplhistory.asp>.
23. <http://www.hammondindiana.com/old_main.html>.
24. <http://www.mtvbrehm.lib.il.us/about-us/copy_of_director-s-message>.
25. R. Anna Morris Clark, 'Women's Literary and Social Clubs of the Black Hills', *Bits and Pieces* 11:1 (1976), 26.
26. Cleo Dolphus Thompson, 'The Portia Club of Payette: Then and Now', <www.portiaclub.com>.
27. <http://www.cityofdenton.com/index.aspx?page=381>; Stella L. Christian, *The History of the Texas Federation of Women's Clubs* (Houston: Dealy-Adey-Elgin, 1919), 172–73.
28. 'Woman's Shakespearean Club Celebrates its Anniversary', *Barnesville News-Gazette*, 10 September 1896, clipping from Loula Kendall Rogers papers, Robert W. Woodruff Library, Emory University.
29. Carl K. Bennett, 'The Librarian of a Small Library', Paper read at the Mankato meeting of the Minnesota Library Association, *Minnesota State Library Commission Library Notes and News* 1 (December 1904), 3.
30. For the details of this story, I am grateful to Frank Mowery, Head of Conservation at the Folger Shakespeare Library, who restored the Folio for the club and helped design a special case and room in the Dallas Public Library. See also Michael V. Hazel, *The Dallas Public Library: Celebrating a Century of Service, 1901–2001* (Denton: University of North Texas Press, 2001), 177, 219.
31. *Shakespeariana* 1 (1883), 159.
32. *Shakespeariana* 5 (1888), 29, 264.
33. *Shakespeariana* 5 (1888), 415.
34. Clark, *The Woodland Shakespeare Club*, 9.
35. Douwe Draaisma, *Metaphors of Memory: A History of Ideas About the Mind*, transl. Paul Vincent (Cambridge: Cambridge University Press, 1995), 207.
36. Louis B. Wright, 'Shakespeare for Everyman', *Proceedings of the American Philosophical Society* 106:5 (1962), 393–400 (p. 399). For discussion of the function of memorization and recitation in the nineteenth century, see Catherine Robson, 'Standing on the Burning Deck: Poetry, Performance, History', *PMLA* 120:1 (January 2005), 148–62.
37. Michael Frisch, *A Shared Authority: Essays on the Craft and Meaning of Oral and Public History* (Albany: SUNY Press, 1990), 27.

38. *Shakespeariana* 1 (1883), 29.
39. *North San Antonio Times*, 21 January 1982, clipping from San Antonio Shakespeare Club Folder, VF-SA 4004657, The Daughters of the Republic of Texas Library, The Alamo.
40. Clark, *The Woodland Shakespeare Club*, 19, 21.
41. Frances A. Wittick, 'Founders' Day 1946', MS, Peoria Historical Society.
42. MS, Folger Shakespeare Library, Scrapbook 258624. From a clipping dated 1949.
43. Kate Flint, 'Women and Reading', *Signs* 31:2 (2006), 513.
44. *Shakespeariana* 5 (1888), 312. *The Shakespeare Birthday Book* was edited by Mary F. P. Dunbar, published by Thomas Whittaker in 1883. *Shakespeare Forget-me-nots: A Text Book of Shakespeare Quotation* was published in New York by E.P. Dutton in the 1880s.
45. Kristin L. Hoganson, *Consumers' Imperium: The Global Production of American Domesticity, 1865–1920* (Chapel Hill, NC: University of North Carolina Press, 2007), 123.
46. Personal communication.
47. Katherine Ott, Susan Tucker, and Patricia Buckler, 'An Introduction to the History of Scrapbooks', in *The Scrapbook in American Life*, ed. Susan Tucker, Katherine Ott, and Patricia Buckler (Philadelphia, PA: Temple University Press, 2006), 8.
48. Judy Giles, *The Parlour and the Suburb: Domestic Identities, Class, Femininity and Modernity* (Oxford and New York: Berg, 2004), 22.
49. Leigh Anne Palmer points out that 'the sheer number [of scrapbooks] dedicated to Shakespeare that are preserved in the Folger Library's collection remains a very real reminder of his popularity in America in this period'. See '"A thing of shreds and patches": Memorializing Shakespeare in American Scrapbooks', in *Shakespeare in American Life*, ed. Virginia Mason Vaughan and Alden T. Vaughan (Washington, DC: Folger Shakespeare Library, 2007), 145.
50. Ellen Gruber Garvey, 'Scissorizing and Scrapbooks: Nineteenth-Century Reading, Remaking, and Recirculating', in *New Media, 1740–1915*, ed. Lisa Gitelman and Geoffrey B. Pingree (Cambridge, MA: MIT Press, 2003), 210, 214.
51. S. J. Kleinberg, 'Gendered Space: Housing, Privacy and Domesticity in the Nineteenth-Century United States', in *Domestic Space: Reading the Nineteenth-Century Interior*, ed. Inga Bryden and Janet Floyd (Manchester: Manchester University Press, 1999), 143.
52. See also *American Home Life, 1880–1930: A Social History of Spaces and Services*, ed. Jessica H. Foy and Thomas J. Schlereth (Knoxville, TN: University of Tennessee Press, 1992).
53. *Michigan State Library Bulletin* 1 (May 1896), 33.
54. Paul Connerton has argued that 'images of the past and recollected knowledge of the past [...] are conveyed by (more or less ritual) performances', and that performative commemorative ceremonies work to construct 'social memory'. See his *How Societies Remember* (Cambridge: Cambridge University Press, 1989), 4–5.
55. Connerton, *How Societies Remember*, 40.
56. Connerton, *How Societies Remember*, 44–5. Connerton uses Lukes's definition of ritual as a 'rule-governed activity of a symbolic character which draws the attention of its participants to objects of thought and feeling which they hold to be of special significance'.
57. Personal communication.
58. David Thelen, 'Memory and American History', *The Journal of American History* 75:4 (March 1989), 1117.
59. Maurice Halbwachs, *The Collective Memory* (New York: Harper and Row, 1980), 80.

Chapter 6
Shakespeare and 'Native Americans'
Forging Identities through the 1916 Shakespeare Tercentenary

Monika Smialkowska

In the context of American celebrations of the three-hundredth anniversary of Shakespeare's death, the connection between Shakespeare and Native Americans is not as far-fetched as it may first seem. In one play staged for the occasion, the Bard actually met Native Americans as we define them now: characters who in the past would have been called 'Indians'.[1] Moreover, the term 'native Americans' at the beginning of the twentieth century carried different connotations to the ones it carries now. It was used to refer to those Americans who were descended from the early Northern European (mainly British or 'Anglo-Saxon') colonisers, as opposed to the newer immigrants from Southern and Eastern Europe and other allegedly inferior ethnic groups.[2] Amidst the mounting anxiety about the increased 'new immigration' to the United States, the debates surrounding the ways in which American identity should be defined – what made one a 'native' American – were highly pertinent in the year of the Shakespeare Tercentenary.[3]

As recent critical accounts by Thomas Cartelli and Coppélia Kahn demonstrate, American celebrations of the Tercentenary responded to those debates by joining the efforts of Progressivist reformers to integrate the 'new immigrants' into American society through edu-

Notes for this section begin on page 90.

cation and cultural enrichment.[4] Cartelli and Kahn suggest that this integration programme, while ostensibly egalitarian, in fact promoted a cultural hierarchy biased in favour of the allegedly superior 'Anglo-Saxon' norms of the established American elites. They describe the process in terms of an interpellation of 'the cultural – and racial – Other [...] into Anglo-American culture' and 'an internal or domestic colonizing venture that seeks to enlist the consent and participation of the masses in their enforced acculturation'.[5] However, as useful as these interpretations are, they stem from an almost exclusive focus on the centrepiece of the American Tercentenary celebrations: Percy MacKaye's mammoth 'community masque' entitled *Caliban by the Yellow Sands*, which arguably was to some extent set in motion by members of metropolitan social elites.[6] As I have argued elsewhere, a more complex picture emerges if one looks beyond *Caliban* to consider the countless large and small-scale tributes produced for the Tercentenary across the United States: pageants, masques, plays, exhibitions, lectures, sermons, garden and tree plantings, even Shakespeare parties. These celebrations were, by and large, initiated, organised, and financed by non-governmental groups and private individuals, many of whom did not belong to Anglo-American elites. My initial, broad overview of these events has indicated that the Shakespeare Tercentenary in America was more than just a centrally managed, top-down affair promoting the cultural hegemony of dominant social groups. It provided an arena for negotiating a variety of identities on national and local levels. It also gave some underprivileged groups within American society access to an empowering cultural discourse.[7]

This chapter extends this investigation by examining three neglected Shakespeare Tercentenary contributions, produced in Georgia, Massachusetts, and North Dakota. In addition to a number of smaller tributes, these three North American states put on substantial dramatic performances composed especially for the occasion. Like MacKaye's *Caliban*, these productions belonged to the tradition of pageantry, which enjoyed enormous popularity in America at the time.[8] True to the pageantry form, they combined verbal, musical, and visual elements: speeches, dialogues, processions, songs, dances, and elaborate costuming. Moreover, their texts were published and survive to this day, providing a wealth of information about the Shakespeare celebrations outside of the metropolitan centre of New York.

Local Celebrations: Georgia, Massachusetts, and North Dakota

Atlanta, GA put on the largest of the three events: a great outdoor pageant and masque, staged at the Grant Field stadium on 27 May 1916.[9] The pageant consisted of nine episodes, each presenting either Shakespeare's contemporaries – Queen Elizabeth with her court and the key poets of the period – or various groups of Shakespearean characters: tragic, pastoral, comical, as well as royalty, knights, fairies, and villains. The historical characters served to introduce the Renaissance as the period of supreme artistic achievement, with Shakespeare as its epitome. Meanwhile, the scenes featuring Shakespearean characters exemplified typical behaviours of different kinds of his dramatic personae, for example aggressive banter between swaggerers such as Falstaff, Sir Toby Belch, and Sir Andrew Aguecheek, and romantic pronouncements from lovers such as Miranda and Ferdinand. The pageant episodes were followed by the allegorical masque of 'Time Unmasked', in which Shakespeare's genius, through the agency of his characters, conquered devouring Time. The whole entertainment culminated in Shakespeare's apotheosis: 'the nine Muses crown him with bays and [...] make low obeisance to him, while all the characters of the pageant [...] lift up their hands and shout: Hail! Shakespeare!'[10]

The event produced in Wellesley, a small town twelve miles west of Boston, MA was similar in design, though more modest in scale. It took the form of a masque, entitled *Will o' the World*, which was performed at Dana Estate on 13 May 1916.[11] It was composed of a Prologue, six episodes, and an Epilogue. Like Atlanta's production, it included Shakespeare's contemporaries, characters from his plays, as well as allegorical and mythological figures. While employing the episodic structure similar to the Atlanta event, *Will o' the World* introduced a slightly tighter overall plot. Each episode revolved around a perceived stage in Shakespeare's life: 'Shakespeare the Child', 'Shakespeare the Lad', 'Shakespeare the Playwright', 'Shakespeare the Father', and 'Shakespeare the Dreamer'.[12] Each presented an imaginary situation influencing Shakespeare's poetic career. Those included encounters with historical figures (Shakespeare's children, Queen Elizabeth, Ben Jonson, Walter Raleigh, and Francis Bacon), as well as episodes such as Shakespeare witnessing the Kenilworth entertainment of 1575, and grieving for the death of his son. Out of these events arose flashes of poetic inspiration, including visions of Shakespearean characters, among them Puck, Portia, Desdemona, Othello, Shylock, Jessica, and Ariel. In the final episode – 'Shakespeare Today'[13] – Shakespeare was transported to 1916, encountered the audience of the entertainment, and was driven off in an automobile to see the modern world, with its skyscrapers, moving pictures, and the disturbing glimpses of the war raging in Europe.[14]

Grand Forks, ND also offered a masque, entitled *Shakespeare, the Playmaker*. It was created by the Sock and Buskin Society, the University of North Dakota's drama club, while being open to those outside the academic community. It was performed twice – on 12 and 13 June 1916 – at the outdoors Bankside Theatre on campus. Apart from the prologue, interlude, and epilogue, the masque consisted of two main parts. These two, like *Will o' the World*, staged imaginary episodes from Shakespeare's life. The first, set in 1588, presented Queen Elizabeth's visit to Greenwich Castle, where she was 'welcomed by the country folk with rustic entertainment'.[15] The key part of this entertainment consisted of a play devised by the yet unknown Shakespeare, based on the *Pyramus and Thisbe* episode from *A Midsummer Night's Dream*. The second part, taking place about twenty years later, showed Shakespeare and Ben Jonson at a May fair at Gravesend, encountering some travellers returning from the New World, who bring with them not only amazing stories and a Native American painting, but also two American Indians. This episode led to a medley of scenes from *The Tempest*, apparently arising from Shakespeare's creative engagement with the New World material. The overall structure of the masque charted the progress of Shakespeare's artistic career from his 'earliest efforts [...] as an unknown craftsman', to 'the mature achievement of the playmaker'.[16]

As these brief outlines demonstrate, the three entertainments shared many common features: the format and trappings of pageantry, outdoor setting, large cast, and the introduction of both Shakespeare's contemporaries and his dramatis personae as characters. All three were amateur enterprises, involving local communities as producers, participants, and audiences. Moreover, as the following discussion will demonstrate, all three engaged in constructing and debating various interrelated – and sometimes conflicting – identities: national, local, ethnic, social, and cultural.

National Identity

While the *Literary Digest* called the Shakespeare Tercentenary 'a celebration which is not primarily patriotic',[17] its specifically American character was, in fact, emphasised in various ways. Some commentators pointed out that, because of the war in Europe, America was the only place where Shakespeare could be honoured properly.[18] Others, like Pauline Periwinkle, went even further, claiming that 'there is a quality attaching to the American recognition of the Shakespearean Tercentenary that even British celebrants can not [sic] possess. It is comparable to the extension of the Gospel message to the gentiles'.[19] This, according to Periwinkle, was due to America adopting the English language and being on the forefront of offering its benefits, epitomized by Shakespeare, to its diverse constitutive ethnic groups: 'not Anglo-Saxons and Celts alone are legatees of this store of intellectual and spiritual wealth, but mankind of every race and blood emerge from America's melting pot joint heirs of this matchless treasure'.[20] Periwinkle concludes: 'The nationalizing significance of this tercentenary movement should appeal to every American who is a genuine patriot'.[21] The combination of Shakespeare and Americanisation is further illustrated in a letter which Miss Gertrude Walker wrote to Percy MacKaye in 1916: 'I have been writing a Shakespearean pageant to be given in connection with a homecoming celebration by the city of Racine [...]. The conception requires a dance to symbolize the American flag'.[22] Clearly, the Bard and American national symbols could be made to go hand in hand.

One common way to link Shakespeare and America during the Tercentenary celebrations was to use *The Tempest*, considered 'Shakespeare's one American Play',[23] as a master narrative. *The Tempest* provided a 'magical' space where anything was possible, as the Wellesley entertainment suggested:

> 'Tis Prospero's isle here, where may come to pass
> Whatever will; not recking time or space
> Stratford or Wellesley [...].[24]

Moreover, the play offered a framework for staging an encounter between Shakespeare's England and the New World. This is clearly seen in the North Dakota entertainment, whose director, Frederick Koch, singled out *The Tempest* as 'the play with which our masque is chiefly concerned'.[25] Not only does Shakespeare's meeting with the Transatlantic travellers in the second part of the masque result in his envisioning of scenes from *The Tempest*, but the ideas of the New World expansion permeate the whole piece. In the first part, on the eve of the Spanish Armada, Sir Francis Drake prophesies: 'England yet will win for herself a place upon the seas and in the New World.'[26] In the Interlude, the Chorus announces that 'England's spirit', which conquered the Armada, also 'found its way / To waiting lands beyond the sea!'.[27] This could be considered an unquestioning praise of Englishness and, by extension, of Anglo-American hegemony. However, as Koch explains in his introduction, the masque envisions 'a new heaven and a new earth for Elizabethan England'.[28] This apocalyptic language implies a radical transformation, rather than an unbroken continuation. America is a new world, in which national, cultural, and social identities will have to be forged anew.

Local Identities

While the Drama League of America instigated and promoted the national Shakespeare Tercentenary celebrations, it explained from the beginning that its role was purely 'initiatory and co-ordinating'.[29] The preparation of particular events was left to the numerous grassroots organisations and individuals across the country. The League's aim was to 'organize local celebrations all through every city, in the local groups that already exist, and then bring them to a focus in some large municipal festival in which the whole city can have a part'.[30] Consequently, Tercentenary activities across the U.S. became local affairs, responding to the needs of specific communities and generating neighbourhood involvement and civic pride.[31]

This comes across very clearly in the texts and the publicity surrounding the entertainments discussed here. In *Will o' the World*, the location of its performance – Wellesley, Massachusetts – slips into the fiction of the masque in an almost uncanny manner. The first episode of the piece presents Leicester entertaining Queen Elizabeth at Kenilworth Castle in 1575.[32] However, when the Queen asks 'What is here, my lord?', Leicester's puzzling answer is: 'This is a learned town that we approach. / There is a woman's college here, my liege'.[33] This is clearly no longer Kenilworth but Wellesley, as the subsequent dialogue demonstrates. The Queen exclaims in surprise: 'A woman's college! Never have I heard / Of such a thing!' – to which Leicester replies: ''Tis Wellesley, in the shire / Of Norfolk'.[34] Without warning, the action of the masque is transported in space and time to the here and now of the masque's production. Curiously, Queen Elizabeth does not seem to notice this transformation, nor does Leicester explain it. The Queen responds to the introduction of Wellesley, in the shire of Norfolk, by saying: 'Good old names', connecting them implicitly to English tradition.[35] It is as if the 'good old England' of her time seamlessly merged into the present day of a small New England town. However, there is one more twist in the conversation. Leicester comments on the fact that the street is 'strangely hard', which elicits an enthusiastic response from Elizabeth:

> A street so paved in a small country town!
> Wonder of wonders! London would do well
> To pave her streets so, too! 'Tis passing strange!
> This thing so near, and I knew not of it![36]

In one deft stroke, Wellesley surpasses Elizabethan London, a provincial town upstages the metropolitan centre and, by implication, America outdoes England. Furthermore, the last sentence posits a complicated relationship between the American periphery and the English centre. The little American town of Wellesley is 'so near', yet the English ruler had been ignorant of it. This statement implies a closeness and easy continuity between the English traditions and the New World. At the same time, however, it confers the power of supreme knowledge, together with the supreme achievement indicated in the previous lines, on the provincial American town, rather than on the English capital.

The local character of the Atlanta celebrations comes out most clearly in the publicity surrounding the event. The *Atlanta Constitution* went so far as to strike a competitive note, declaring: 'Other cities which have presented similar pageants this year have, in nearly every case, had to import their talent [...] but the Drama league has worked out the Atlanta pageant entirely as a home affair'.[37] It is worth noting that by 'the Drama league' the article means the local branch, rather than the nationwide organisation: a few sentences before, the author says that the pageant is being organised 'under the auspices of the Atlanta Drama league, and with the co-operation and indorsement [sic] of practically every civic organization'.[38] Moreover, the fact that the event was entirely a 'home affair' seemed so important to the local press that it was singled out as 'one of the most remarkable features of the celebration and one of which Atlanta should be justly proud'.[39] The newspaper proceeded to state that 'there was not a single feature of the presentation which was not entirely an Atlanta product', and declared: 'nothing has ever been staged in Atlanta which was more typically Atlantan than the Shakespearean tercentenary of Saturday afternoon'.[40] One may be forgiven for thinking that the characters of the pageant, such as Queen Elizabeth, Raleigh, Marlowe, Jonson, and Shakespeare himself, were unlikely candidates for being 'typically Atlantan'. However, by producing the entertainment locally, Atlanta was able to claim them as her own, as if making them her honorary citizens.

In fact, the definition of an 'Atlantan' adopted for the occasion seems to have been quite capacious. The article quoted above calls Armond Carroll, the author of the entertainment's text, 'an Atlantan', but he was a relative newcomer to the city.[41] According to the *Atlanta Constitution*, he 'was born in Asheville, N. C., [...] reared in Shelby, N. C., and Pittsburgh, Pa. He prepared for college at Mount Harmon school, Massachusetts, and spent a year at Yale. [...] He came to Georgia in 1911'.[42] It seems that it was not deemed necessary to have been born and bred in Atlanta to qualify as its native. It was enough to be resident in the city and make a valuable contribution to its life. In this respect, it is interesting that one of the civic organisations endorsing the Atlanta pageant was the Council of Jewish Women.[43] Together with this ethnic minority, the event attracted a wide spectrum of the city's social classes: 'the pageant and the masque were participated in by people in all circumstances and from every walk of life. The rich and the poor alike joined in the great celebration'.[44] These facts go against the reading of the Tercentenary as an affair orchestrated by Anglo-American social elites with the aim of enforcing the cultural hegemony of that cultural strand.

However, there was one social group that did not seem to have been included in Atlanta's grand Shakespeare celebrations: African Americans. The coverage in the *Atlanta Constitution* does not record their participation in the masque and pageant.[45] Moreover, an event reported in the newspaper suggests that the occasion was white-orientated:

> An interesting incident connected with the pageant was the introduction of Henry B. Walthall, whose reputation as the 'Booth of the "Movies"' was borne out in his superb acting in the 'Birth of a Nation'. He was introduced as 'a man who has rendered the south a distinguished service in portraying her sufferings in the days of the reconstruction', and he was greeted with a great ovation.[46]

It is unlikely that a man who had played a leader of the Ku Klux Klan in a notoriously racist film would have been applauded by an audience including significant numbers of African Americans. The references to that movie and to the South's 'sufferings in the days of the reconstruction' indicate viewers sympathetic to the Klan rather than to Black Americans. This is borne out by Othello's role in the pageant. He has a non-speaking part, and is introduced, together with Desdemona, with the words: 'The dark Moor, and she so white / Who was strangled, Day by Night'.[47] It appears that the inclusive character of the event did not extend to African American Atlantans.

Similar to the Atlanta celebrations, the North Dakota event's local character was emphasised more in the supplementary material surrounding it than within the masque itself. The prefatory statements by Frederick Koch, the Professor of Drama at the University of North Dakota, under whose direction the entertainment was produced, insist on its unique and innovative character: 'The idea is original in conception [and in] manner of composition'.[48] This originality lies chiefly in the masque's communal authorship, which takes a step further the ideas of 'community drama' propagated by Percy MacKaye.[49] While MacKaye's *Caliban by the Yellow Sands* aimed to be 'a drama *of* and *by* the people, not merely *for* the people', its text was written by MacKaye himself.[50] *Shakespeare, the Playmaker*, on the other hand, was 'designed and written by a group of twenty students at the University of North Dakota', which, in Koch's words, 'reassured us that [...] not only can the people participate as actors in a community play, but [...] can actually *create* a drama democratic – a new art-form of the people, embodying their own interpretation of life'.[51] In this respect, the provincial entertainment surpasses the one produced in the metropolitan centre by the most vocal proponent of community drama.

In an article published simultaneously with the first publication of the masque, Koch expands on his views regarding the nature of the local community. He discusses the home-grown talent which produced the success of the Shakespeare celebration (and of the entire dramatic movement at the University of North Dakota) in terms of breeding naturally from the local land. He proudly calls one of the authors of the pageant's epilogue 'a North Dakota boy, a son of the prairie'.[52] He applies similar language to another contributor, Ethel H. Halcrow: 'She is a true child of our soil, endowed with its limitless life, and with the inherent sense of beauty of her prairie home, visioning, perhaps, something of the promise of our Western plain to translate its pioneer forces into a new art of the people, adequate, democratic'.[53] And he extends this organic metaphor to all North

Dakota University amateur thespians, calling them 'practically the first generation of Americans from the soil, from our prairie pioneers', whose efforts 'promis[e] much toward a genuinely native art yet to come'.[54] Interestingly, this association of 'genuinely native art' with the prairie soil does not, for Koch, exclude newer immigrants. Elsewhere, he comments on *Shakespeare, the Playmaker* and another pageant produced two years earlier: 'These communal dramas were designed and written entirely [...] by a group of students [...] at the University, representing the various races – English, Scandinavian, Russian, Polish, Bohemian, Irish, Scotch, German, Italian – that have gone into the making of our big state'.[55] It seems that in order to be a native of North Dakota, it is by no means necessary to hail from the 'Anglo-Saxon' stock. It is perfectly possible to spring out of the prairie soil as a first-generation, yet 'native', American.

Koch's inclusive model of North Dakotan – and American – identity becomes more complicated when one takes into consideration the Native Americans (by today's definition of the term) who appeared in the masque. As mentioned before, in the second part of the entertainment, Shakespeare meets two American Indians, brought to England by the travellers coming back from the New World. The Indians were played by two Chippewas from the nearby reservation, Marchebenus (Flying Eagle) and Temoweneni (Little Boy).[56] If anybody had a rightful, autochthonic connection to the Dakotan prairie, it was surely them, its original inhabitants. However, American Indians are the one group conspicuously absent from Koch's list of 'the various races [...] that have gone into the making of our big state'. Instead, they are treated as an exotic curiosity both in the text of the masque and in the surrounding commentary. In the masque, William Strachey admits that the natives whom he brought to England 'do in stature greatly resemble white men', but he presumes that 'Further inland, no doubt, they become more distorted until their human semblance is quite destroyed'.[57] Similarly, Ben Jonson pronounces: 'We wis not of what wild orgies these monster men are capable'.[58] The Indians can communicate with the English only through an interpreter, and their own language is rendered almost inhuman in the stage directions.[59] They 'respond to their interpreter's request with grunts of approval' and, on seeing a painting of the legendary Native American monster Piasa, they 'walk toward the picture, uttering strange, guttural sounds'.[60] Thus, rather than becoming partners in a meaningful dialogue, they are reduced to an exotic spectacle: they are met with 'exclamations of wonder', and they 'dance for the crowd a native dance'.[61]

Koch's commentary on the masque displays a similar attitude: he calls the American Indians 'specimens of the strange inhabitants of the new world'.[62] His other phrases treat the Indians either instrumentally: 'We shall use full blooded Chippewas from the Turtle Mountain Reservation', or as possessions: 'our own native red men'.[63] Moreover, it is not clear whether the word 'native', when applied to the Indians, means quite the same thing as in Koch's phrase 'genuinely native art', discussed above. The Indians' art – a dance and a painting – gets admitted into the masque, but it is rendered voiceless and strange, a spectacular but alienated backdrop to the main action. While recognised and, to some extent, included in the celebrations, the Indians – unlike the English, the Poles, or the Italians – remain on the margins of American society, a position embodied in reality by their removal to the reservation.

Conclusion

An examination of the American celebrations of the Shakespeare Tercentenary other than its New York centrepiece reveals that they participated in a negotiation of a complex network of interrelated identities. On the national level, Americans were reclaiming what they saw as their English Renaissance heritage, but not without asserting that they had to rework, renew, and improve on the original. Engagement with Shakespeare could provide cultural legitimation for some underprivileged groups, such as the lower classes, Jews, and new immigrants.[64] Other groups, however, found themselves in ambivalent positions: either incorporated into the narratives of American origins as the exotic 'other' (like the American Indians in North Dakota), or excluded from mainstream celebrations (like the African Americans in Atlanta). Locally, the Tercentenary served as a focal point for the expression of civic pride and the promotion of regional interests, not always identical to those of the metropolitan centre. Overall, Shakespeare celebrations of 1916 provided an arena in which the ideas regarding what made one a 'native' American could be debated, contested, and reworked.

The Native Americans with the painting of Piasa. I have been unable to determine conclusively whether the character on the left depicts Shakespeare or one of his contemporaries present in that scene. Photo courtesy of the University of North Dakota Theatre Arts archive.

Monika Smialkowska is a Senior Lecturer in Early Modern Literature at Northumbria University. Her current research explores the ways in which the three-hundredth anniversary of Shakespeare's death in 1916 was commemorated across the world. She has published book chapters and journal articles on the topic, and she has edited a special issue of *Shakespeare* on 'Shakespeare and the Great War'. She is working on a monograph about the 1916 Shakespeare Tercentenary, and co-editing, with Edmund King, a collection of essays entitled *Memorialising Shakespeare: Commemoration and Collective Identity, 1916-2016* (forthcoming with Palgrave).

Notes

1. Lyle M. Bittinger et al., *The Book of Shakespeare, the Playmaker, Written in Collaboration by Twenty Students of The University of North Dakota, Under the Direction of Professor Frederick H. Koch of the Department of English, Designed for the Shakespeare Tercentenary Commemoration by The Sock and Buskin Society, for Presentation at The Bankside Theatre on the Campus of The University of North Dakota* (Grand Forks, ND: University of North Dakota, 1916, repr. from *The Quarterly Journal of the University of North Dakota*, 6:4 (July 1916), 56. Hereafter referred to as *Shakespeare, the Playmaker*.
2. See, for example, Madison Grant, *The Passing of the Great Race, or The Racial Basis of European History* (New York: Charles Scribner's Sons, 1916), 74, 77.
3. John Higham, *Strangers in the Land: Patterns of American Nativism 1860–1925* (1955. Rpt. New York: Atheneum, 1963), 106–93; Matthew Pratt Guterl, *The Color of Race in America, 1900–1940* (Cambridge, MA: Harvard University Press, 2001), 14–67.
4. Thomas Cartelli, *Repositioning Shakespeare: National Formations, Postcolonial Appropriations* (London and New York: Routledge, 1999), 63–83; and Coppélia Kahn, 'Caliban at the Stadium: Shakespeare and the Making of Americans', *Massachusetts Review*, 41:2 (2000), 256–84.
5. Resp. Kahn, 'Caliban at the Stadium', 268; and Cartelli, *Repositioning Shakespeare*, 75.
6. Percy MacKaye, *Caliban by the Yellow Sands: Shakespeare Tercentenary Masque* (Garden City, NY: Doubleday, Page & Co, 1916).
7. Monika Smialkowska, '"A democratic art at a democratic price": The American Celebrations of the Shakespeare Tercentenary, 1916', in *Transatlantica* (2010:1), http://transatlantica.revues.org/4787, accessed 10 December 2018.
8. Under the label of 'pageantry' I include both related forms of the pageant and the masque. For comprehensive accounts of the development of American pageantry in the period, see David Glassberg, *American Historical Pageantry: The Uses of Tradition in the Early Twentieth Century* (Chapel Hill, NC: University of North Carolina Press, 1990); and Naima Prevots, *American Pageantry: A Movement for Art and Democracy* (Ann Arbor, MI: U.M.I. Research Press, 1990).
9. Armond Carroll, *A Pageant and Masque for the Shakespeare Tercentenary* (Atlanta, GA: Atlanta Center, Drama League of America, 1916). A headline in the local newspaper indicates the scale of the event: 'Over 2,000 People Will Take Part in Elaborate Pageant on May 27, in Honor of the Shakespeare Tercentenary' (*Atlanta Constitution*, 21 May 1916, C10).
10. Armond Carroll, *A Pageant and Masque for the Shakespeare Tercentenary*, 77.
11. Isabelle Fiske Conant, *Will o' the World: A Shakespearean Tercentenary Masque* (Wellesley, MA: Mangus Printing, 1916).
12. *Will o' the World*, 17–19.
13. *Will o' the World*, 19.
14. *Will o' the World*, 38–41.
15. *Shakespeare, the Playmaker*, 9.
16. *Shakespeare, the Playmaker*, 7. This explanation comes from the short introductory article 'Communal Play Making', included in the published text of the masque (7–8). It was written by Professor of Drama Frederick H. Koch, under whose direction the entertainment was produced.

17. 'The Shakespeare Community Masque', *Literary Digest*, 10 June 1916, 1700–1701 (p. 1701).
18. MacKaye, 1916, xiii.
19. Pauline Periwinkle, 'Tercentenary of Death of Shakespeare in April', *Dallas Morning News*, 3 April 1916, 13.
20. Pauline Periwinkle, 'Tercentenary of Death of Shakespeare in April', 13.
21. Pauline Periwinkle, 'Tercentenary of Death of Shakespeare in April', 13.
22. Gertrude G. Walker, letter to Percy MacKaye, 19 April 1916, in 'Papers of MacKaye Family', ML-5 (108), Rauner Special Collections Library, Dartmouth College, Hanover, NH. Courtesy of Dartmouth College Library.
23. '"Tempest" to Have a Notable Revival', *New York Times*, 27 March 1916, 9.
24. *Will o' the World*, 22.
25. Koch in *Shakespeare, the Playmaker*, 8.
26. *Shakespeare, the Playmaker*, 26.
27. *Shakespeare, the Playmaker*, 37.
28. *Shakespeare, the Playmaker*, 9.
29. Percival Chubb, 'The Shakespeare Tercentenary: Developments of the Plan for a Nation-Wide Celebration', *The Drama: A Quarterly Review of Dramatic Literature* 19 (August 1915), 531–36 (p. 535).
30. 'New York Gets Ready to Honor Shakespeare', *New York Times Magazine*, 19 March 1916, SM12.
31. The Drama League of America was a voluntary organisation which arose from women club activities. It had fairly autonomous local branches across the country. See Karen J. Blair, *The Torchbearers: Women and Their Amateur Arts Associations in America, 1890–1930* (Bloomington and Indianapolis, IN: Indiana University Press, 1994), 148–60.
32. *Will o' the World*, 17–18 and 24–25.
33. *Will o' the World*, 24.
34. *Will o' the World*, 24. Wellesley, Massachusetts, in Norfolk County, is home to Wellesley College, a female higher education institution established in 1870.
35. *Will o' the World*, 24.
36. *Will o' the World*, 24.
37. 'Over 2,000 People Will Take Part in Elaborate Pageant on May 27, in Honor of the Shakespeare Tercentenary', *Atlanta Constitution*, 21 May 1916, C10.
38. *Atlanta Constitution*, 21 May 1916, C10.
39. 'Thousands Witness Beautiful Pageant', *Atlanta Constitution*, 28 May 1916, D1, D8 (D8).
40. Ibid.
41. Ibid.
42. 'Armond Carroll Is Author of Shakespearean Pageant', *Atlanta Constitution*, 16 April 1916, 4.
43. 'Guarantors Being Sought for Shakespearean Pageant', *Atlanta Constitution*, 4 May, 1916, 4.
44. 'Thousands Witness Beautiful Pageant', 8.
45. In other locations, African-Americans held their own Tercentenary events, separate from the mainstream ones (see my discussion in 'A democratic art'). It is possible that this was also the case in Atlanta. More research needs to be conducted to gather evidence for this.
46. 'Thousands Witness Beautiful Pageant', 8.

47. Armond Carroll, *A Pageant and Masque for the Shakespeare Tercentenary*, 26.
48. *Shakespeare, the Playmaker*, 7.
49. Community theatre was MacKaye's long-standing project, on which he published extensively. His views on the issue at the time of the Shakespeare Tercentenary are neatly summarized in the Preface to *Caliban by the Yellow Sands*, xiii-xxiii.
50. MacKaye, 1916, xviii.
51. *Shakespeare, the Playmaker*, 7 (emphasis in the original).
52. Frederick H. Koch, 'The Amateur Theater in the University', *The Quarterly Journal of the University of North Dakota*, 6:4 (July 1916), 298–308 (p. 307).
53. Koch, 'The Amateur Theater in the University', 301.
54. Koch, 'The Amateur Theater in the University', 298.
55. Frederick H. Koch, 'The Dakota Playmakers', *The Quarterly Journal of the University of North Dakota*, 9:1 (October 1918), 14–21 (p. 14).
56. *Shakespeare, the Playmaker*, 17.
57. *Shakespeare, the Playmaker*, 55.
58. *Shakespeare, the Playmaker*, 56.
59. Before the production of the masque, Koch explained that the Native Americans 'will speak their own language thru an interpreter' ('The Amateur Theater', 307).
60. *Shakespeare, the Playmaker*, 56. A footnote in the text explains: 'Piasa is the name given to a prehistoric rock painting formerly on the face of a bluff on the Mississippi river, near the present city of Alton, Illinois, and first discovered by Marquette in 1673' (49). For the monster's description by the seventeenth-century French Jesuit missionary, Jacques Marquette, see *Father Marquette's Journal*, trans. Reuben G. Thwaites, ed. Roger L. Rosentreter, 3rd ed. (Lansing, MI: Michigan Historical Center, 2001), 30–31. A modern reconstruction of the painting is now a tourist attraction in Alton, IL (<http://www.altonweb.com/history/piasabird>, accessed 10 December 2018).
61. *Shakespeare, the Playmaker*, 56.
62. 'The Amateur Theater', 305.
63. 'The Amateur Theater', 306–307.
64. Lawrence W. Levine, *Highbrow/Lowbrow: The Emergence of Cultural Hierarchy in America* (Cambridge, MA: Harvard University Press, 1988), 176.

Chapter 7

The Disciplines of War, Memory, and Writing
Shakespeare's *Henry V* and David Jones's *In Parenthesis*

Adrian Poole

A True Englishman in 1916

The *Book of Homage* assembled by Israel Gollancz to mark the tercentenary of Shakespeare's birth unequivocally hailed 'the greatest Englishman'. Coppélia Kahn interprets this Shakespeare as 'the signifier of an autochthonous English identity, an Englishness that is self-authorized and racially pure'. The very purpose of the *Homage* was 'to assert the continuity of a single national identity, "England" from the mediaeval past to the imperial present, by invoking Shakespeare'.[1] The mediaeval past is a convenient point of origin for this dream narrative of English identity, memorably embodied in good King Henry V, 'the mirror of all Christian kings'.[2] Or as the Bishop of Oxford and Regius Professor of Modern History (1866–84), William Stubbs put it, speaking of the real historical figure, 'one of the greatest and purest characters in English history. [...] A true Englishman'.[3]

For the Homagers who refer explicitly to the war in which they were engulfed, Henry V provides a natural rallying-point, along with John of Gaunt's speech about '[t]his happy breed of men, this little

Notes for this section begin on page 105.

world'.[4] Most rampantly, Lionel Cust, of Eton and Trinity College, Cambridge, Director of the National Portrait Gallery (1895–1909): 'in every part of the globe, wherever the English heart beats true, Shakespeare's words ring as loud and true to-day as they did when King Henry V first spoke them on the boards of the Globe Theatre'. Like Glendower calling spirits from the vast deep, Cust asks his readers to draw inspiration in their hour of need from the spirit in whom Poet and Warrior King seem indistinguishable.[5]

An Anglo-Welshman in 1916

> In certain stages of society, in tribal communities especially among some peoples, the *poeta* not only had a recognized status along with the makers of other necessary works, but occupied a special position essential to the structure of that society, for he was the official 'rememberer', and continuator of the tradition of that tribal organism.[6]

David Jones spent much of his artistic life trying to commemorate the complex and elusive tradition of a tribal organism. Where now was the 'tribe' to be found? The object of his quest was more than the land to which he felt he belonged, more than the comradeship forged in the Great War. It was lodged in the idea of a 'Wales' that had retained its independence through the anglicizing centuries since the death of the last King Llywelyn in 1282. Jones looked back to the ancient scattered 'Celtdom' out of which the Welsh nation was born, and further back still behind Celtdom itself, through the Fall and the Rise of the Roman *imperium*, into the dark backward and abysm of time.[7] In terms of his art, what he was trying to remember was 'an essential Celticity'. This is what he hailed in James Joyce ('the most creative literary genius of this century'), an art-form that could be described as 'intricate, complex, flexible, exact and abstract'.[8] These are not quite the terms, or not all of them together, for which one would look to the art-forms we think of as 'Shakespearean'.

Born in 1895 at Brockley in Kent, David Jones was brought up as a Londoner. His ethnic affiliations on his mother's side were English, with an Italian inflection, and on his father's side Welsh. Jones was entranced by his Celtic provenance but also estranged from it; he did not speak Welsh and had difficulty learning it, describing himself with regret as monoglot. With little evident aptitude for anything other than drawing, he joined the Camberwell School of Art at the unusually early age of fourteen, and five years later, on 2 January 1915, he enlisted as a private soldier in the 15th Battalion (London Welsh) of the 23rd Foot, Royal Welch Fusiliers. He served on the West Front from December 1915 to February 1918; he was wounded at the Battle of the Somme in July 1916 but returned to active service the following October. These biographical details give some sense of the distance, in 1916, of a 21-year-old private soldier on the front line, from the circumstances in which Gollancz's expensive, limited edition of the *Homage* was produced and first read.

David Jones and *Henry V*

In Parenthesis was based on Jones's experiences of the war in the first six months of 1916; it was composed from 1928 onward and published in 1937. Jones insisted on calling it simply 'writing'. Divided into seven sections it stages a dizzying parade of voices in verse and prose, and the alternation along the border of verse and prose is crucial. After a raucous, 'barbarous' rendition of a soldier's song we read: 'He reverts to the discipline of prose'. But it is a 'discipline' simmering with barely controlled competing voices: 'Who's kidding – and shorts as well – you ask Sid Whiting at the gum-boot store, straight from the 'major he said ...'.[9]

This writing is as densely allusive as the other two great modernist texts that Jones admired at the time of composition, Eliot's *The Waste Land* and Joyce's *Anna Livia Plurabelle*. Amongst these voices can be heard a great deal of literary quotation and reference, slivers of a collective memory, putative or potential. In *The Great War and Modern Memory* (1975), Paul Fussell gets irritated by the literary allusions. He reads them as confirming the likenesses between this war, the Great War, and all others, and conferring on its participants a nobility borrowed from the past. But Fussell is wrong to claim that Jones invokes the past to glorify the present. Jones proposes that some aspects of war do not change much, such as saying goodbye to your nearest and dearest: 'We are in no doubt at all but what Bardolph's marching kiss for Pistol's "quondam Quickly" is an experience substantially the same as you and I suffered on Victoria platform'.[10] More sonorously, in the magnificent meditation on 'Art in Relation to War', written during the Second World War, Jones speaks on behalf of a generation who had lived through war, and died for real in it: 'We can guess, better than our immediate forebears, something of what a paid foot-soldier at Crécy *felt* about a damp bow-string and the heavy Picardy mud, and the relationship between these immediate, intimate, bodily-known things and the Plantaganet pretensions'.[11]

But the comparison Jones makes between Mr X adjusting his box-respirator and 'I saw young Harry with his beaver on' is a different matter. About the former there is nothing glorious, glamorous, or ennobling; here as elsewhere the memory of Shakespeare is, for Jones, at best rueful, quizzical, humorous, and at times caustically ironic. The radiant Shakespearean memory of young prince Harry draws on Jones's own memory of a hurried exchange in the trenches. Worried about a mate of his, he called out to another friend, 'Have you seen Harry?' and got the hurried reply 'I saw young Harry with his beaver on'. Jones is intrigued by the precarious assumption of a shared cultural knowledge:

> my friend guessed that I should probably know the context of 'I saw young Harry with his beaver on' and it chanced that, in a vague way, I did, but *might well not have done* [original emphasis], for I was [...] not then, nor, for that matter am I now, all that familiar with Shakespeare.

It is true that the shouting friend was 'a cultivated & educated Englishman, but not ... "high brow" – not at all'. Jones draws from the memory of this incident the conviction that 'there was in that war, a sense of re-participating in history'.[12] It is this 'sense' that *In Parenthesis* seeks to re-enact.

In his Preface Jones notes the superficial associations with Shakespeare's *Henry V* aroused by the experience of the Great War. 'No one, I suppose, however much not given to association, could see infantry in tin-hats, with ground-sheets over their shoulders, with sharpened pine-stakes in their hands, and not recall "... or may we cram, / Within this wooden O ..."'. But there were, he says, 'deeper complexities of sight and sound to make ever present "the pibble pabble in Pompey's camp"'.[13] It is this 'pibble pabble' that Jones re-creates. He describes the proliferating diversity of 'every man's speech and habit of mind' as 'a perpetual showing', with a long list of references that juxtapose figures from high cultural official history (Napier, Wellington) and popular insurrection (Jack Cade, John Ball), popular song ('High Germany', 'Dolly Gray') and popular characters (Bullcalf, Wart, and Poins from *Henry IV, Part Two*), modern 'Jingo largenesses' and ancient legendary smallnesses (the Kingdom of Elmet), and so on. The list concludes significantly with 'Coel Hên', the ancient Celtic King who has been anglicized into old King Cole.

But Jones has his eye and ear on what lies behind and beneath – 'the Celtic cycle that lies, a subterranean influence as a deep water troubling, under every tump in this Island, like Merlin complaining under his big rock'.[14] Why 'tump', one wonders? This is a western and west midland word, so the *OED* tells us, related to Welsh *twmp* ('but this may be from English'). In Jones's resonant phrasing, however, it is hard not to hear in 'tump', so close to the 'r' of 'troubling', and indeed of Merlin's 'big rock', some intimation of a last trump, when the deep waters of that Celtic past might rise up.

Memory Unmeasured

Deep waters, deep memories. The seventh and final section of *In Parenthesis* vividly renders the climactic assault by the company whose fortunes we have followed. It is based on the writer's own experiences at the Battle of the Somme on 10–11 July 1916, the assault on Mametz Wood in which many of his friends and comrades died, and the writer was himself wounded. The second paragraph reads thus:

> The memory lets escape what is over and above –
> as spilled bitterness, unmeasured, poured-out,
> and again drenched down – demoniac-outpouring:
> who grins who pours to fill flood and super-flow insensately,
> pint-pot – from milliard-quart measure.[15]

Unmeasured and unmeasurable, insensately and beyond sensation. Only so much can be contained by the pint-pot of an individual memory. But a long written text – like a great parenthesis – can hold more than a pint-pot, can open itself to receive the flood and super-flow of a 'milliard-quart measure'.

The Disciplines of War and Literary Memory

One of the first to die, before the assault has even begun ('zero minus seven minutes') is Lance Corporal Lewis ('who worshipped his ancestors like a Chink / who sleeps in Arthur's lap' – like Falstaff in 'Arthur's bosom').[16] Introduced on page 1, he is one of the characters who lodges most firmly in the reader's memory: 'Temporary unpaid Lance-Corporal Aneirin Merddyn Lewis', we are told, 'had somewhere in his Welsh depths a remembrance of the nature of man'.[17] Lewis is contrasted with the English Corporal Quilter, 'who knew nothing of these things',[18] but also with fellow-Welshmen such as the fiery Watcyn, who 'knew everything about the Neath fifteen, and could sing *Sospan Fach* to make the traverse ring', but 'might have been an Englishman when it came to matters near to Aneirin's heart'.[19] There is another particular Welsh soldier to whom I shall come back. Under enemy fire, we are later told, 'Lance-Corporal Lewis sings where he walks, yet in a low voice, because of the Disciplines of the Wars'.[20] The poet's own note directs us to Shakespeare's *Henry V*, where this is of course Fluellen's mantra. Jones tersely comments: 'Trench life brought that work pretty constantly to mind'.[21] There are other references to 'the Disciplines of War', most notably near the end at Lewis's death.[22] The other-worldly Queen of the Woods brings him a rowan sprig: 'You couldn't hear what she said to him, because she was careful for the Disciplines of the Wars'.[23] When Lewis dies, however, the spirit of Fluellen does not die with him. As rumours about a German counter-assault proliferate and the British troops begin to think about retreating, Captain Cadwaladr 'is come to the breach full of familiar blasphemies', and quashes the rumours: 'Through on the flank my arse'. He restores 'the Excellent Disciplines of the Wars'.[24] Jones is reported to have said, 'There were lots of Fluellens'.[25]

Shakespeare's *Henry V* is only one of many intertexts in *In Parenthesis*, less prominent than Thomas Malory, the *Song of Roland*, and *Y Gododdin*. Nor is it the only Shakespearean reference. There is an extraordinary interfusion of voices, literary and vernacular, 'high and low', bereaved of or freed from any certainty of source or attribution, as here for example when the Sergeant appears to be waking his men at dawn: 'To peel back those either-ducks me slumberin' lovelies – Prince Charming presents his compliments. Who's this John Moores in his martial cloak – get off it, wontcher – come away counterfeiting death – cantcher – hear the bird o' dawnin' – roll up – it's tomorrow alright'.[26] Sleeping Beauty, the real military hero Sir John Moore dead at Corunna in 1809, a mixture of Feste's song 'Come away, come away death' (*Twelfth Night*, 2.4.50–65), Macduff's 'Shake off this downy sleep, death's counterfeit' (*Macbeth*, 2.3.73), and '[t]he bird of dawning' from *Hamlet* (1.1.141). Elsewhere there is the sociable joke on a real advertising slogan for Veno's – 'cures for rough weather' – drawn from Amiens's song in *As You Like It*, 'Here shall he see / No enemy / But winter and rough weather' (2.5.6–8).[27] When Corporal Watcyn complains of being soaked through he gets showered with advice:

> Wring your vest man, there is no enemy here.
> *Veno's*, corporal – cures for rough weather.[28]

This, recall, from a man who claimed to be, like his comrades, not all that familiar with Shakespeare.

Nevertheless, the references to *Henry V* are sufficiently prominent to make one pause over its role in the poem as a whole. In the Preface Jones thinks of his own double heritage and its reflection in the Anglo-Welsh regiment he joined: 'the mind and folk-life of those two differing racial groups [Londoners and Welsh] are an essential ingredient to my theme [...]. These were the children of Doll Tearsheet. Those are before Caractacus was'.[29]

John Barnard has a trenchant essay reporting that Jones's writing helped him to grasp what was wrong with Shakespeare's play, 'its inability to maintain the heroi-comical mode of *1–2 Henry IV*'. According to Barnard the change of direction in *Henry V* that required the death of Falstaff resulted in a botched play. Jones repairs some of the damage by restoring the spirit of Falstaff in the comic humourists, by 'uncovering the epic dignity of the common soldier', and by finding a way 'to praise and elegize their deeds within the disciplines of war, without sentimentality or betrayal. *In Parenthesis*'s perspective is a tragic one'.[30] I have much sympathy with this line of thought but it is curious that Barnard finds nothing to say about the great night-scene before Agincourt. Williams, Bates, and Court make up a very different trio from Pistol, Bardolph, and Nym and they represent a different kind of common soldier. One could easily extend Barnard's argument to say that Jones does justice to the solemn and dignified spirit of Williams and his mates as well as the more rambunctious temper of the Eastcheap crowd.

1282 and All That

But Williams is important to Shakespeare's play in more ways than one. Not only does he supply an unhumorous alternative to Pistol; his relationship with Fluellen is no less crucial, for they are the two key loyalists on whom King Henry's authority depends.

Shakespeare's King Henry wants to dominate not only events but their interpretation and memory. This is an ambition repeated by the dominant critical history, interpretation, and indeed *memory* of his play. But the King cannot do it alone and the play carefully demonstrates the 'collaborations' on which he depends (to stress Diana Henderson's well-chosen word).[31] *In Parenthesis* offers an oblique reading of the King's ambitions by ignoring his voice and point-of-view, and concentrating almost entirely on the multitudinous voices he aspires to master. Jones's whole narrative form de-centres Shakespeare's: the rapid alternation of point-of-view and of voice – both sight and sound – precludes any stable authority.

My contention however is that *In Parenthesis* de-centres not just *Henry V*, not just Shakespeare, but the whole conventional reading of English literary history and culture entailed by Kahn's characterization of the *Homage*'s project: 'the continuity of a single national identity, "England", from the mediaeval past to the imperial present'. *Henry V* is the ideal text through which to effect this because it celebrates the success of the Anglo-Welsh pact on which 'English' and, a fortiori, 'British' identity is founded. The character normally anglicised as 'Fluellen' is crucial to this success, as Terence Hawkes has noted: 'Anglicization could wish for no better advertisement'; he is 'the model Welshman necessary to the project of a united Britain'.[32] And yet a certain anxiety continues to hover around 'Fluellen', if only because at a crucial moment in the play *his memory loses its discipline* and he starts comparing King Henry V to Alexander the Pig, at length.[33]

A certain anxiety also hangs around the other loyalist, the English soldier known as 'Williams' on the page, a name not exactly free from suspicion of Welsh origins. The fact that in performance however he remains entirely unnamed lends him a curious and precious independence, as if his allegiance remained undecided. The naming of 'Fluellen' is a different matter. '[B]rutally reduced', as Hawkes calls it, this is the ghost of the name of the last native-born Prince of Wales, Llywelyn ap Gruffyd, whose death on 11 December 1282, one of Jones's editors tells us, was 'one date in Welsh history that none of David's friends could fail to memorize'.[34] In fact *In Parenthesis* remembers the figure of another legendary Welshman commandeered and vanquished by Shakespeare, the figure of rebellion whom 'Fluellen' is designed to replace: the alternative monarch known to his compatriots as Owain Glyn Dwr.

'man as artist hungers and thirsts after form'[35]

If there *is* a centre to the English tradition created by this poem it is in Malory not Shakespeare. But Malory's 'centrality', if that is the right word, looks back far more than it looks forward. Hence the significance of the pre-'English' poetry, legend, and myth, in the poem's very form, like the Celtic cycle noted above, 'a subterranean influence as a deep water troubling, under every tump in this Island'.

Consider in this respect the title-pages to each of the parts, and to the volume as a whole. Each of the seven parts has a main title drawn more or less directly from literary texts in the dominant English tradition. Thus, Part I: 'The many men so beautiful' (Samuel Taylor Coleridge, 'The Ancient Mariner'); Part 2: 'Chambers go off, corporals stay' (a witty adaptation of a stage-direction and line from *Henry V*, 3.1 and 3.2); Part 3: 'Starlight order' (Gerard Manley Hopkins); Part 4: 'King Pellam's Launde' (Malory); Part 5: 'Squat garlands for White Knights' (an amalgamation of Hopkins and Lewis Carroll); Part 6: 'Pavilions and Captains of Hundred' (Malory, and Historical Books of the Old Testament); Part 7: 'The five unmistakable marks' (Carroll's 'Hunting of the Snark'). These identifications are provided by Jones himself in his Notes. All these titles from diverse sources are partnered by brief epigraphs from a single source, *Y Gododdin*. The effect of these fragments from this sixth-century early Welsh epic poem is of a singular voice – direct in address, devoid of enhancing glamour, as for example, the epigraph to Part I: 'Men marched, they kept equal step [...] / Men marched, they had been nurtured together'; to Part 2: 'On Tuesday they put on their dark blue raiment; / On Wednesday they prepared their enamelled shields'. And so on. The effect is one of rough correspondence to the action and incident represented in each part, except for the very final one: 'Gododdin I demand thy support. It is our duty to sing: a meeting place has been found'. All these extracts are Englished, except for the title-page itself which reads

IN PARENTHESIS
seinnyessit e gledyf ym
penn mameu

The defiance of this *other* language here is partly retracted in Jones's notes where we learn that it means: 'His sword rang in mothers' heads'. This is a female and specifically maternal grief that resonates with some memorable moments in the body of the poem itself, as for example, of the German killed by the grenade: 'He calls for Elsa, for Manuela'.[36] So, a certain 'discipline' is represented by these title-pages and the collaboration of 'English' and 'Welsh' traditions: the former is confident, exuberant, sportive, various, written, while the latter is restrained, elegiac, dignified, singular, sung.

For all the discipline at which these title-pages aim, there is nevertheless a certain unredeemed raggedness to the textual totality that is *In Parenthesis*. It is not, and could never be, quite as finished as its maker would have wished: 'There are passages which I would exclude, as not having the form I desire – but they seem necessary to the understanding of the whole', so he writes.[37] And again: 'I had intended to engrave some illustrations, but have been prevented'.[38] In fact the first edition contained two pictures, a frontispiece and end-piece, which are not reproduced in some paperback editions. My Faber paperback edition of 1963 (1978 impression) has the former on the cover, but not the latter. But even leaving these visual 'addenda' aside, the verbal matter surrounding the body of the writing itself is remarkably prolific. There is a note of introduction by T.S. Eliot; there is Jones's preface; there is his dedication, a little work of art in itself. There is what he calls the prologue, a resonant fragment from the *Mabinogion* about unending traumatic memory. Nor has the reader even yet reached 'the text', for we still have the title-page to Part I, before we have finally arrived at 'the beginning'. Then, when it is all over there are Jones's notes. And then there is a final page for which there is no readily available name, though in the spirit of the poem's pairings it clearly rhymes with the dedication, repeating the capitals: a Benediction perhaps. This speaks not with the voice of the poet but simply with quotations from Scripture, six of them: from the Apocalypse, Leviticus, Isaiah, Exodus, and two from the Song of Songs. These two are themselves a kind of pair, the third and the sixth. The first reads: WHAT IS THY BELOVED MORE THAN ANOTHER BELOVED. The second and last answers this, all the more beautifully for its obliqueness: THIS IS MY BELOVED AND THIS IS MY FRIEND.

Missing in Action

I return in conclusion to the Welshman at the centre of Jones's poem: the soldier known as 'Dai Great-coat'. It has been convincingly argued that the whole narrative is structured around the relation between Dai Great-coat's 'boast' at the very centre of the text in Section 4, and the visionary passage near the end when the Queen of the Woods distributes the flowers to the secret princes, on both sides.[39] Dai Great-coat represents an excess that is the polar opposite or complement to Aneirin Lewis's attachment to the Disciplines of War. Dai is not the only such image of a wilder Welshman than the disciplined Lewis. There is Watcyn who keeps being promoted for bravery, then getting drunk and reduced to the ranks. But Watcyn has no memory, beyond the names of the Neath rugby fifteen and the words of 'Sospen Fach'. Dai Great-coat, who 'articulates his English with an alien care', is a different matter. The memories represented by his 'boast' span western history and legend; Jones tells us he associates it with 'the boast of Taliessin at the court of Maelgwen'.[40] If we were to look for a Shakespearean equivalent to Dai Great-coat, comparable to the one between Lewis and Fluellen, where would we go? To Glendower, of course. Yet this is emphatically not an equation made by Jones's text. There are plenty of Shakespearean Fluellens, but there is no equivalent to Shakespeare's Glendower because Jones is reaching behind and beneath to a legendary figure that resists anglicization or even proper naming at all: something extravagant, something beyond or outside official history or memory, something – we might say – immemorial.

Why is Dai Great-coat missing from the scene of final benediction by the Queen of the Woods? His great boast in Part 4 contains the challenge: 'You ought to ask: Why, / what is this, / what's the meaning of this'.[41] Jones associates his essay on 'Art in Relation to War' with the same legendary requirement:

> Because the Land is Waste ... it [this writing] seeks to do what the hero in the myth was rebuked for not doing, i.e. it seeks to 'ask the Question'. Although, alas, unlike the myth, it does not suppose that in asking the question the land can be 'restored'. Although if all the world asked the question perhaps there might be some fructification – or some 'sea-change'.[42]

If the Queen of the Woods provides a kind of answer to 'the Question', then it is one that Dai is unable or unwilling to receive: 'Dai Great-coat, she can't find him anywhere – she calls both high and low, she had a very special one for him'.[43]

It is intriguing in this context to read Diana Henderson's analysis of the two submerged historical figures in Shakespeare's *Henry V*, the Welsh loyalist Davy Gam, esquire (aka Dafydd ap Llywelyn of Brecon), one of the mere four men 'of name' on the English side to die at Agincourt (4.8.99), and the French Queen Isabel (or Isabeau) of Bavaria, who presides over the espousal of English King and French princess.[44] Henderson remembers for us some of the historical realities that Shakespeare's play takes pains to gloss over or suppress, including the threat of a Franco-Welsh alliance that shadowed the imperial designs of the English. These two figures are as essential to the play's 'comic resolution' as the fictional Dai Great-coat and the Queen of the Woods are to Jones's narrative, but the 'collaboration' amenably provided by Davy and the foreign queen is not quite matched by Jones's pair. Beyond nationality but on French ground, Jones's Queen of the Woods unites all the beautiful dead young men, German, English, and Welsh, including Aneirin Lewis. But where is Dai Great-coat? As the popular song with which his boast had ended goes:

> Never die never die
> Never die never die
> Old soljers never die
> Never die never die
> Old soljers never die they never die
> Never die
> Old soljers never die they
> Simply fade away.[45]

Upon the crowing of the cock, the bird of dawning? Old soldiers never die, and if they fade away, perhaps they fade into something rich and strange, in the subterranean waters troubling every tump, ready to rise again, as in the great Celtic myths of return.

This has taken us some distance from Shakespeare but that has been my point, and Jones's point, about the uses and the limits of Shakespeare for the creative artist writing in English, particularly when it comes to the representation of matters as uncontrollable as war and memory, even by the strictest artistic discipline.

Adrian Poole is Emeritus Professor of English Literature at the University of Cambridge, and a Fellow of Trinity College. He has written extensively on Shakespeare, especially on the tragedies, and on the afterlives of Shakespeare in the work of later artists, writers and readers, including *Shakespeare and the Victorians* (Arden, 2003), the series *Great Shakespeareans* in 18 vols. (Bloomsbury, 2011–14, co-edited with Peter Holland), and an essay on 'Shakespeare in 1816', in *Celebrating Shakespeare: Commemoration and Cultural Memory*, eds. Clara Calvo and Coppélia Kahn (Cambridge, 2015). He has also written on Charles Dickens, George Eliot, Thomas Hardy, Robert Louis Stevenson, and Henry James, and his wider interest in the novel is represented by the *Cambridge Companion to English Novelists* (2009).

Notes

1. Coppélia Kahn, 'Remembering Shakespeare Imperially: The 1916 Tercentenary', *Shakespeare Quarterly* 52 (2001), 457, 459.
2. *Henry V*, Chorus 2.0.6. Unless otherwise noted, all citations of Shakespeare's plays are from *The Norton Shakespeare*, ed. Stephen Greenblatt, Walter Cohen, Jean E. Howard, and Katharine Eisaman Maus, 2nd edn. (New York: W. W. Norton, 2008).
3. William Stubbs, *The Constitutional History of England*, vol. III (Oxford: Clarendon Press, 1878), 75.
4. *Richard II*, 2.1.45.
5. *A Book of Homage to Shakespeare*, ed. Israel Gollancz (Oxford: Oxford University Press, 1916), 103.
6. 'Notes on the 1930s', in *The Dying Gaul and Other Writings*, ed. Harman Grisewood (London and Boston: Faber and Faber, 1978), 46–47.
7. *The Dying Gaul*, 56–57.
8. *The Dying Gaul*, 58.
9. David Jones, *In Parenthesis* (London and Boston: Faber and Faber, 1978), 103.
10. *In Parenthesis*, xv.
11. *The Dying Gaul*, 58.
12. From a draft letter to Bernard Bergonzi, quoted by Jonathan Miles, *Backgrounds to David Jones: A Study in Sources and Drafts* (Cardiff: University of Wales Press, 1990), 85.
13. *In Parenthesis*, xi. Fluellen's words, *Henry V*, 4.1.71.
14. *In Parenthesis*, xi.
15. *In Parenthesis*, 153.
16. *Henry V*, 2.3.10.
17. *In Parenthesis*, 1–2.
18. *In Parenthesis*, 2.
19. *In Parenthesis*, 89.
20. *In Parenthesis*, 42.
21. *In Parenthesis*, 196.
22. *In Parenthesis*, 42, 78, 117, 172, 181, 186, as noted by John Lee, 'Shakespeare and the Great War', in *The Oxford Handbook of British and Irish War Poetry*, ed. Tim Kendall (Oxford: Oxford University Press, 2007), 134–35.
23. *In Parenthesis*, 186.
24. *In Parenthesis*, 181.
25. Thomas Dilworth, *Reading David Jones* (Cardiff: University of Wales Press, 2008), 91.
26. *In Parenthesis*, 60.
27. Lee, 'Shakespeare and the Great War', 151.
28. *In Parenthesis*, 71.
29. *In Parenthesis*, x.
30. John Barnard, 'The Murder of Falstaff, David Jones and the "Disciplines of War"', in *Evidence in Literary Scholarship*, ed. René Wellek and Alvaro Ribeiro (Oxford: Clarendon Press, 1979), 31, 22.
31. Diana E. Henderson, *Collaborations with the Past: Reshaping Shakespeare across Time and Media* (Ithaca, NY, and London: Cornell University Press, 2006), 202–58.
32. Terence Hawkes, 'Bryn Glas', in *Post-Colonial Shakespeares*, ed. Ania Loomba and Martin Orkin (London and New York: Routledge, 1998), 133. See also *Shakespeare*

and Wales: From the Marches to the Assembly, ed. Willy Maley and Philip Schwyzer (Farnham: Ashgate 2010).
33. *Henry V*, 4.7.9–42.
34. *Dai Great-Coat: A Self-portrait of David Jones in His Letters*, ed. René Hague (London and Boston: Faber and Faber, 1980), 23.
35. *The Dying Gaul*, 134.
36. *In Parenthesis*, 169.
37. *In Parenthesis*, x.
38. *In Parenthesis*, xiii.
39. Resp. *In Parenthesis*, 79–84 (Dai Great-coat's 'boast'); and 185-6 (Queen of the Woods). See also Dilworth, *David Jones*, 93.
40. See Jones's note 37, *In Parenthesis*, 207–10.
41. *In Parenthesis*, 84. See also Jones's note M, *In Parenthesis*, 210.
42. *The Dying Gaul*, 124.
43. *In Parenthesis*, 186.
44. Henderson, *Collaborations*, 207, 217.
45. *In Parenthesis*, 84.

Chapter 8
Monumental Play
Commemoration, Post-war Britain, and History Cycles

Anita M. Hagerman

> Bring forth the body of old Salisbury,
> And here advance it in the market-place,
> The middle centre of this cursed town.
> Now have I paid my vow unto his soul.
> For every drop of blood was drawn from him
> There hath at least five Frenchmen died tonight.
> And that hereafter ages may behold
> What ruin happened in revenge of him,
> Within their chiefest temple I'll erect
> A tomb wherein his corpse shall be interred,
> Upon the which, that everyone may read,
> Shall be engraved the sack of Orleans,
> The treacherous manner of his mournful death,
> And what a terror he had been to France.[1]

First by enacting bloody vengeance and then by building a monument, Talbot repackages and, to use modern parlance, remarkets the corpse of Salisbury as a new, psychological English weapon. What is being memorialized is not Salisbury, however, but the 'ruin that happened in revenge of him'. This reminds us that while monuments stand, they always signify more than simple remembrance of their putative object of commemoration. Providing energy as valuable to an army as firepower, as valuable to a man as his life, the prime benefits of monumentalizing belong to the builder.

Notes for this section begin on page 118.

Commemoration is not limited to literal stone monuments in the play. When at the time of Salisbury's death Talbot swears to the French, 'I'll be a Salisbury to you!' he is vowing to embody his comrade's memory in his own actions, a fact predicated at its root upon the remembrance of those actions.[2] Burgundy promises to do the same for Talbot, declaring, 'Warlike and martial Talbot, Burgundy / Enshrines thee in his heart, and there erects / Thy noble deeds as valour's monuments'.[3] Burgundy, of course, is a turncoat, so his monument to Talbot will prove to be built not on the stone foundations of a pre-existing 'chiefest temple' such as that Talbot promises to Salisbury, but on the unreliable sandy ground of his French heart. But Talbot, in point of fact, does not need Burgundy to memorialize him; the play itself is his monument. Thomas Nashe's reference to a Talbot play (probably *1 Henry VI*) in *Pierce Penniless* makes just this point. Nashe praises chronicle plays for commemorating greatness, providing a monument to heroes past 'wherein our forefathers' valiant acts (that have line long buried in rustic brasse and worme-eaten bookes) are revived'.[4] Just as Talbot, and not Salisbury, embodies the 'terror of the French', the artistic triumph that Elizabethan plays represent, not the heroes they portray, perpetuate the glory of the nation. This is one of the ways Shakespeare's histories are 'monumental plays', and it is an interpretation as old as the plays themselves.

Cycle performances of the histories, which have become surprisingly frequent in the last fifty years, make these plays monumental in size as well as in aspect. Scholars often hail the Royal Shakespeare Company's 1964 'Wars of the Roses' history cycle as a *sine qua non* of history cycle performance.[5] Undoubtedly, the 1960s was the decade in which the history cycle was established as a modern theatrical phenomenon. Within the space of only a few years in the mid-60s, several history cycles were staged. Important Italian and German cycles quickly followed the RSC's 'Wars' (in 1965 and 1967, respectively), so that by the end of the decade, staging a cycle, while still rare, was hardly an unheard of event. But these were not the earliest cycles: that distinction belongs to a German production by Franz von Dingelstedt in 1864.[6] Over the next century, there were many productions of linked history plays, primarily in Germany, but a few in Britain, most of which have only begun to be discussed critically. Commemoration is a recurring feature of these productions: from Dingelstedt to the RSC, producers have used the occasion of a commemorative moment as an opportunity to present a history cycle. The 1864 and 1964 cycles were staged to commemorate Shakespearean anniversaries, whereas the 1951 productions, which are the focus of this chapter, were aligned with the more obliquely relevant Festival of Britain, a national celebration commemorating the half-century as well as the centennial of another celebration, the 1851 Great Exhibition.[7] That history cycles have their roots in commemorative occasions is interesting. What is even more remarkable, however, is what is being commemorated, what purpose that commemorating serves, and how that context affects our approach to the histories today.

This chapter focuses on two very different productions from 1950s England, when the Birmingham Repertory Theatre ('Rep') and the Shakespeare Memorial Theatre (SMT) staged contrasting history cycles to coincide with the 1951 Festival of Britain. The Rep, led by the ground-breaking Sir Barry Jackson, presented *Henry VI, Part Two*, in 1951, expanded by 1953 to a *Henry VI* trilogy using a single cast, director, and design. Meanwhile, the SMT in Stratford-upon-Avon, under the artistic leadership of the conservative Sir Anthony Quayle, produced the entire second tetralogy with overlapping casts and design, but three different directors. These festival cycles reflected key differences in the companies' philosophies, politics, and financing, but they both benefited from surprisingly similar underpinnings. The two Festival of Britain cycles shared an approach to the histories that combined theatrical novelty with conventional literary heritage, providing an opportunity to self-aggrandize through commemoration. Stratford was certainly unique in the magnitude of its deference to Shakespeare, but the Rep's project relied just as strongly on Shakespeare's iconic status and on the cultural capital of commemoration. Companies produced cycles because they could claim that the subject matter was of importance to national identity, and also because they could parlay that importance into their own campaigns for increased national prestige (and external subsidy). It is therefore significant to explore how the history cycle emerged not only as *part* of, but *because of* a culture of commemoration.

Shakespeare's Histories: Identity and Commemoration

It is not within the scope of this essay to recount a detailed history of the linking of Shakespeare's history plays into cycles, but it is worth noting that even the earliest imaginings of cycle performances mix the plays' perceived unity, national identity, and commemoration.[8] Graham Holderness places the beginning of cycle-think at least as early as the editing of the 1623 Folio (itself a commemoration to Shakespeare by his friends) when the reordering and re-titling of the plays according to royal chronology made it possible for readers to conceive of the plays as one extended narrative, even if the playwright had not.[9] Later, the Romantics on both sides of the channel championed the history cycle: Coleridge imagined them as the basis for a celebratory, even quasi-religious experience, suggesting that '[i]t would be a fine national custom to act such a series of dramatic histories in orderly succession every Christmas holiday'.[10] Coleridge's cycles, had they existed, would have fostered a new trinity of nationhood, Shakespeare, and God. Over the centuries, Shakespeare's histories have provided a pivotal locus of national identity formation both in Britain and, perhaps surprisingly, abroad as well. What John Joughin calls the 'Shakespearean mediation of the national' has been a feature of British national identity since the plays were written, as Holderness and Murphy have illustrated; but it is a much wider, international phenomenon as well, as several recent studies have begun to explore.[11]

The process by which the history plays became particularly attractive sites of theatrical nation-making is an anthropological one in which performance is used to legitimize a national ideal. When narratives are harnessed to do the work of staging national identities, the artists working with those narratives are at once indebted to history while creating a new version of that history for present day consumption. Kiki Gounaridou sees in this process an almost irresistible historical revisionism in which 'nations create a "neo-classical" culture in order to construct a new version of their national cultural identity'.[12] To Joughin, this process is reciprocal and reflective: 'The formation of a national culture is dependent upon, and often invokes, a particular version of the past which it would then either reaffirm or deny'.[13] The Festival of Britain history productions invoked different versions of Britain's past. For the Rep, *Henry VI* 'offered a vision of Lions tearing the country apart over the crown'.[15] In contrast, the SMT's second tetralogy presented a celebration of orthodox Tudor historical thought in keeping with the patriotic tradition. But despite employing different visions of Britain, an essential constant was their turn to Shakespeare. Stuart Hampton-Reeves notes the conservatism of the choice:

> As the past was scoured for elements which could constitute a new de-imperialized history to drive Britain into the future, Shakespeare presented an unarguable figure of achievement, recognized nationally and internationally and [...] a true 'living memory' in which the past could be translated into the currents of the future.[16]

These cycles thus adopt the past to construct a new version of their national identity twice over. First, they reinforce Shakespeare as a national icon. Second, they embrace the plays themselves as relics of the Elizabethan age, a period considered to be the theatrical high point that companies wish to commemorate and emulate. The universalizing impulse of the Shakespeare myth was paradoxically co-opted in the case of the histories by a concurrent emphasis on defining the national self.

The history cycle therefore occupied a fertile location at the intersection of nostalgia, art, and identity. But while pageant-heavy history cycles had been a common feature of the German stage for nearly a century, British performances were rare and largely academic before the 1950s. What had changed? In his seminal study on modernism and national culture, 'A Shrinking Island', Jed Esty describes mid-century England as taking an 'anthropological turn' in response to the 'shrinking' of English influence.[17] As postwar, post-Empire, devolutionary England could no longer see itself as a universal culture, even within Britain, Esty argues, it was forced to see itself as one culture among many, and this prompted an obsession with national identity and a subsequent 'rise of an Anglocentric culture paradigm'.[18] Applying Esty's reading of culture to history cycles, we see that they respond to two impulses: an inclination to look inward as a result of the new urgency to define national identity, and an Anglocentric desire to affirm Shakespeare's universal appeal. For theatre producers looking for material relevant to the Festival of Britain, a nationwide commemorative event intended specifically to reconnect the country with a sense of national identity, the histories were a valuable commodity.

Thus, theatre companies that produced history cycles were able to draw upon the plays' perceived national importance in order to bolster their own cultural status, which they felt increasing pressure to do given the economic shift to subsidized theatre in the '50s and '60s. As the conditions of production were shifting, the commemorative occasion of the Festival of Britain created an opportunity to literalize the postwar 'anthropological turn' on stage, and Shakespeare's histories provided the mechanism to do so. Thus, economic, political, and cultural pressures of postwar Britain coalesced, and the history cycle entered the repertoire of the professional British stage.

Festival of Britain Cycles

In 1951, Britons were not only experiencing the dissolution of the Empire, but also dealing with the effects of extended rationing of consumer goods, governmental economic restrictions, and housing shortages. The Festival wanted to signal the end of postwar doldrums and the beginning of a new era, bolstered by technological advances and British ingenuity.[19] It purported to be nationalist, patriotic, and unifying, and under its auspices communities were called upon to celebrate Britain in a manner that showcased their own strengths. The Rep and SMT used the Festival to kick off history cycle projects despite the obvious discrepancy between the content of the plays and the Festival's stated goal of celebrating 'the story of British contributions to world civilisation in the arts of peace'.[20]

The paradox was most pronounced with the Rep's choice. As Hampton-Reeves remarks, the Birmingham trilogy 'traded on the unresolved, incomplete and fractured nature of a country traumatized by power politics'.[21] But *2 Henry VI*, which seems an ill-suited choice to celebrate Britain's past, was in another sense quite apt: it was obscure. The play is only inappropriate if one presumes the object of commemoration and celebration is Britain; it fits better if that object is Shakespeare himself and, by extension, the theatre company that is restoring the Shakespearean canon to its fullest potential. Indeed, the Rep championed the quality and Shakespearean authorship of the *Henry VI* plays, which many saw as righting a wrong committed by 'the Shakespearean critic and the Shakespearean scholar who have had their way far too long', scaring theatres away from the plays by denigrating their quality, or 'because doubt ha[d] been cast on their parentage'.[22] The *Birmingham Post*'s reviewer was one of many who applauded Jackson for having 'rescued' the plays 'from an obscurity entirely undeserved'.[23] If we accordingly adjust our perspective of the Rep's Festival of Britain performances slightly, away from expecting a patriotic celebration, which the plays challenge, and focus instead on the productions as an artistic celebration, we find ourselves on excitingly fertile ground. The Rep was not interested in celebrating the Wars of the Roses as a glorious moment in Britain's past; rather, they found a striking and original way to celebrate their own artistic skill and obtain a higher standing in the theatrical establishment.

The Rep's policy, as printed in its playbills, had been to focus not on serving the demands of the commercial theatre, but rather on 'serving the art'. Therefore, the Rep required subsidy, and to win subsidy, they needed to be seen as vital to national culture. Choosing rarely performed works and presenting them on such a large scale was a direct attempt to garner attention for the quality of the Rep's work, as well as to encourage additional support for the arts up north generally. Jackson staged the *Henry VI* plays when no company in London would take the chance. Indeed, the Old Vic imported the Rep's trilogy to complete their five-year Shakespeare programme in 1953. Jackson wanted the Rep to be a national institution, representing and speaking to the average Briton, separate from what many saw as the elitism of London.[24]

This was an uphill battle, made more difficult by the proximity of Stratford. In a letter to the *Birmingham Post* (run under the title 'This is Shakespeare Too') self-described 'regular Shakespeare-goer' Fay Davis complains about Birmingham's difficulties in drawing the size of audience that Stratford regularly did.[25] Davis blames the audiences themselves, who prefer Stratford-upon-Avon's bardolatry and star power to Birmingham's artistry:

> Now that the Stratford Festival has commenced, we read once more of the devotees who queue for hours, prompted, they would have us believe, by their intense interest in the drama and not because it is fashionable to go to Stratford, nor because of the 'star' attractions. The Birmingham Repertory Theatre is at present giving an admirable production of 'Henry the Sixth, Part Two' [...]. But are these Shakespeare enthusiasts flocking to Station Street to do homage to the Bard? No, they do not appear to have heard that this rarely performed play is being given, for last week there were many empty seats.[26]

Davis's complaint reflects a fundamental difference between the Rep and the SMT: Stratford could rely on the audience it had been building up for generations, even if some attended, according to Davis, for 'sheer affectation and hero-worship'. But Birmingham's choice to stage Shakespeare constituted a direct challenge to Stratford, and they therefore traded every bit as heavily on Shakespeare's iconic status, just as they also shared an indebtedness to the cultural capital of commemoration.

While Birmingham was presenting the more unexpected work for the Festival year, the SMT tellingly staged the less financially risky second tetralogy. Whereas Birmingham presented itself as an urban, Labour-centred alternative to London, the SMT's home of Stratford-upon-Avon was the pastoral, conservative alternative. The SMT had long promoted Stratford as a commemorative heritage site, and also as the home of the (self-proclaimed) pinnacle of Shakespearean performance expertise. Ivor Brown describes the SMT's mission as explicit monumentalizing, both for the company and their house playwright. They hoped

> to carry Stratford to the world and make its company what Shakespeare would have called a 'blazon' for the dramatic genius, for the poetry, and for the language of the man himself, and also for the quality of the British stage.[27]

By presenting the second tetralogy as a cycle, the SMT raised the bar on production size: at the time no other theatrical institution had the infrastructure to produce professional theatre on this scale. They were showing off, trumpeting (justifiably) the infrastructure they had built, the audience base Birmingham could only envy, and their own artistic merit and skill.

Both companies argued their own importance by claiming to be fixing a problem. For the Rep, it was restoring the early histories to the repertoire. For Quayle, it was restoring them to what he argued was their proper form: a cycle. Although Quayle was committed to the commercial theatrical model, he villainised it here, portraying it as the entity that had obscured the 'epic' he argued the second tetralogy was meant to be:

> Successful theatrical practice over a great number of years had stealthily built a mountain of misrepresentation and surrounded it with a fog of ignorance [...]. [O]ur purpose in presenting the History Cycle was to rediscover and try to reveal the author's true intentions.[28]

Quayle saw the SMT as uniquely situated to correct the failure of history and economics that had led Shakespeare's histories to be seen as individual works: 'The plays have come to be thought of as separate entities since the economic and organizational difficulties in the way of presenting the cycle as a whole are so formidable'.[29] He hoped to show that the SMT's status and skill could meet any organisational challenges. Novelty, combined with the occasion of the Festival, would overcome economic difficulties by attracting sufficient funds through investors and ticket sales.

Whereas the Rep challenged the preconception that the *Henry VI* plays were unstageable, the SMT suggested that the plays of the second tetralogy are *more* difficult to stage – that they demand a cycle production – and anything less was perpetrating a crime against Shakespeare and patriotism. In a companion volume to the SMT's Festival production, J. Dover Wilson insists that the focus of this cycle was to study the tetralogy's unity, not its politics, and he sees the production as nothing short of a heroic rescuing of Shakespeare's great epic from the ravages of history.[30] Nevertheless, the SMT's production was deeply political because it was straightforwardly and uncritically patriotic in its insistence on defending the ideal, traditional, national hero. Dover Wilson argues that a cycle restores Henry of Monmouth to the person of a 'young and ardent knight' who can not be judged harshly because of his youth.[31] For the SMT and Dover Wilson, the cycle form not only recovers a lost, truer Shakespeare, but preserves Henry V as 'the mirror of all Christian kings' and 'Star of England'. Their claim therefore links the history cycle to national identity on a clearly patriotic level; moreover, it situates the SMT as the best institution through which to celebrate that identity.

As different as the politics and approaches to the histories were between the Birmingham and Stratford-upon-Avon productions, what is shared between these Festival of Britain cycles is their recognition of the histories' function as monumental plays linked with national identity, as well as the common understanding that the history cycle could be a distinctly valuable commodity in a commemorative context. In short, these companies saw the history cycle as 'event theatre': something important but rare, something worth travelling to see, something worth paying to support.

Indispensable Unstageability and the Persistence of Commemoration

At the core of the history cycle 'event theatre' rhetoric is a paradoxical argument I call 'indispensable unstageability', or theatre companies' arguing that the histories are indispensable to Britain's theatrical greatness, but are at the same time so difficult to stage that only a top-quality, subsidized theatre could do so.[32] Indispensable unstageability was a mixture of stage bravado and rebranding of the histories. The early histories were now declared by companies to be excellent playtexts instead of weak plays, texts that show not an unseasoned playwright or a collaborative effort, but the work of a young, vigorous writer who wrote well for the stage, even if scholars had noted the plays' artistic inadequacies. The later histories were also rebranded, their long performance history described as inadequate because it failed to reflect the extended narrative of the cycle. This new theatrical perspective on the histories shifted the perception of them from their being notably *inferior* texts to their being notoriously *difficult* texts. In contemporary history cycle productions, companies tend to reinforce the idea of the plays' unstageability while staging them, arguing implicitly that to perform the unperformable deserves support. In other words, theatre companies argue that the histories are indispensable because they want to make *themselves* indispensable. It is therefore not surprising that the commemorative focus of history cycles has been the companies themselves as much as it has been national identity or Shakespeare.

The Royal Shakespeare Company's 1964 'Wars of the Roses' more firmly than any other production established the rhetoric of indispensable unstageability that still surrounds cycle productions of the histories. But in fact, the RSC's 'Wars' was repeating the pattern established by the 1951 cycles. How the RSC managed to make themselves indispensable monuments to Shakespeare is a direct result of the commemorative functions of these early post-war cycle performances. Under Quayle, the SMT had proudly proclaimed its ability to operate without taking public money, but by the early 1960s, the company, now under the more experimental leadership of Peter Hall and renamed the Royal Shakespeare Company, was vehemently pursuing subsidy for itself as a national ensemble theatre on the model of the Berliner Ensemble. After several difficult seasons trying to make the new structure a success, Hall cancelled the planned season for 1963 and replaced it with 'The Wars of the Roses', an adaptation of the first tetralogy into a trilogy. It was a history cycle intended as an attention-getting coming out party for the newly formed company. Peter Hall explained that 'in the fight to establish the company, we *had* to be in the newspapers every day of the week if possible'. Hall hoped, as Jackson at Birmingham had a decade before, that the novelty of seeing the *Henry VI* plays done well would convince audiences of the cultural value of the theatre company which could manage such a seemingly impossible feat. The 1963 trilogy was then revived in 1964 to be performed alongside the plays of the second tetralogy for special cycle performances in celebration of Shakespeare's 400th birthday.[33] As a further publicity move, the RSC presented all three plays in one day on the anniversary of the Battle of Bosworth. The 'Wars' was thus a triple monument: to Shakespeare in an anniversary year, to the Battle of Bosworth on its anniversary, and – even though the name change and restructuring had in fact happened several seasons earlier – to the RSC itself at its 'birth'.

Hall's venture was successful, and the influence and critical acclaim of this production dwarfed the 1951 cycles. In 1991, Irving Wardle called it 'the greatest Shakespearean event within living memory', and most discussion of the histories in performance recognize the importance of this production.[34] Indeed, since then, the RSC has staged more history cycles than any other company, and the histories have become, as one reviewer noted, 'the stomach on which they march'.[35] These subsequent productions have continued the pattern of linking history cycle productions with commemorative events: company anniversaries, new theatre openings, the millennium, and so forth. In each case, programmes and marketing campaigns argue indispensable unstageability by stressing the project's exciting novelty, sheer scale, and critical contribution to maintaining the national heritage.

Given the cultural implications of the histories, it is reasonable that when theatre companies have presented the histories as a cycle, they have employed them to advance a particular agenda. More surprising, however, is how consistent this agenda has tended to be. The lasting effects of the 1951 Festival of Britain cycles on the imagining of Shakespeare's histories are as much a result of the occasions of their productions, which aligned the histories with commemoration, as of the gravitas or ingenuity of their interpretations. What emerged from the post-war decades was an idea of history cycles as 'event theatre', ideal projects for celebratory, commemorative occasions. This layer of extra-dramatic spectacle led to the sense of occasion that has become associated with the history cycles and has enabled theatre companies to use these monumental plays as a proving ground for their own reputations.

Anita M. Hagerman holds a PhD in English Literature from Washington University in St. Louis and teaches literature, linguistics, and writing at John Burroughs School in St. Louis, Missouri. She has published articles on baroque theatricality, the Stuart court masque, and the cultural politics of Shakespeare in performance. She is also a professional freelance bass player with a particular interest in classical and early music.

Notes

1. Shakespeare, *Henry VI, Part One*, ed. Edward Burns, Arden Shakespeare, Third Series (London: Wadsworth, 2000), 2.2.4–17.
2. *Henry VI, Part One*, 1.4.106.
3. *Henry VI, Part One*, 3.2.118–20.
4. Quoted in Samuel Schoenbaum, *William Shakespeare: A Documentary Life* (Oxford: Clarendon, 1975), 120.
5. See, for example, Dennis Kennedy's generally accepted observation that despite the many earlier performances in Britain and elsewhere, only the RSC's 1964 cycle 'changed common notions of the histories'. In 'Foreword' to *Shakespeare's History Plays: Performance, Translation and Adaptation in Britain and Abroad*, ed. Ton Hoenselaars (Cambridge: Cambridge University Press, 2003), 5.
6. For more on Dingelstedt's production, see Ton Hoenselaars, 'Shakespeare's History Plays in Britain and Abroad', in *Shakespeare's History Plays*, 9–34; Robert K. Sarlos, 'Dingelstedt's Celebration of the Tercentenary: Shakespeare's Histories as a Cycle', *Theatre Survey* 5 (1964), 117–31.
7. The staging of the histories in 1864 also served to commemorate the foundation of the Deutsche Shakespeare-Gesellschaft in that year, an event appropriately planned on the occasion of the Shakespearean anniversary.
8. See *Shakespeare and National Culture*, ed. John J. Joughin (Manchester: Manchester University Press, 1997); Richard Helgerson, *Forms of Nationhood: The Elizabethan Writing of England* (Chicago: University of Chicago Press, 1992); Michael Dobson, *The Making of the National Poet: Shakespeare, Adaptation and Authorship, 1660–1769* (Oxford: Oxford University Press, 1992); and Margreta de Grazia, *Shakespeare Verbatim: The Reproduction of Authenticity and the 1790 Apparatus* (Oxford: Oxford University Press, 1991).
9. Graham Holderness, *Shakespeare: The Histories* (New York: St. Martin's Press, 2000), 2; for an overview of the critical history of 'cycle-think', see 7–12.
10. Samuel Taylor Coleridge, *Coleridge's Shakespeare Criticism*, ed. Thomas Middleton Raysor, 2 vols. (London: Constable, 1960), I: 126. On the Romantics, see *The Romantics on Shakespeare*, ed. Jonathan Bate (London: Penguin, 1992).
11. Graham Holderness and Andrew Murphy, 'Shakespeare's England: Britain's Shakespeare', in *Shakespeare and National Culture*, ed. Joughin, 19–41. For international performance histories, see Hoenselaars, *Shakespeare's History Plays*; Wilhelm Hortmann, *Shakespeare on the German Stage* (Cambridge: Cambridge University Press, 1998); Anthony B. Dawson, 'International Shakespeare', in *Cambridge Companion to Shakespeare on Stage*, ed. Stanley Wells and Sarah Stanton (Cambridge: Cambridge University Press, 2002), 174–93.

12. Kiki Gounaridou, 'Introduction' to *Staging Nationalism: Essays of Theatre and National Identity*, ed. Kiki Gounaridou (Jefferson, NC: McFarland & Company, 2005), 1.
13. Joughin, 1.
14. Stuart Hampton-Reeves, 'Shakespeare, *Henry VI* and the Festival of Britain', in *A Companion to Shakespeare and Performance*, ed. Barbara Hodgdon and W. B. Worthen (Oxford: Blackwell, 2005), 285–96 (p. 291).
15. Graham Holderness, *Cultural Shakespeare: Essays in the Shakespeare Myth* (Hatfield: University of Hertfordshire Press, 2001), 39–40.
16. Hampton-Reeves, 295.
17. Jed Esty, *A Shrinking Island: Modernism and National Culture in England* (Princeton: Princeton University Press, 2003), 1.
18. Ibid., 2.
19. Michael Frayn, 'Festival', in *Age of Austerity*, ed. Michael Sissons and Philip French (Westport, CT: Greenwood Press, 1976) analyzes the Festival *as* a festival, recounting its development, exploring its upper-middle-class origins and perspective. Frayn concludes that while the Festival generated both public enjoyment and profits, it was unsuccessful as a national narrative, because it was never quite clear about what it was celebrating. I also recommend Becky Conekin, *The Autobiography of a Nation: The 1951 Festival of Britain* (Manchester: Manchester University Press, 2003).
20. Festival souvenir programme, quoted in Stuart Hampton-Reeves, 'Shakespeare, *Henry VI*, the Festival of Britain', 287.
21. Hampton-Reeves, 288.
22. Unsigned review of *Henry VI, Part Three*, by William Shakespeare, directed by Douglas Seale, Birmingham Repertory Theatre, Birmingham, *Birmingham Post*, 9 April 1952.
23. Unsigned review of *Henry VI, Parts One, Two, and Three*, by William Shakespeare, directed by Douglas Seale, Birmingham Repertory Theatre, Birmingham, *Birmingham Post*, 17 June 1953.
24. A major London-based production would not be attempted for another 60 years, by which time nearly a dozen successful productions of the first tetralogy plays had been staged. The honor of that London-based production goes to the Globe Theatre's 2013 *Henry VI* trilogy, again chosen commemoratively, as part of the lead-up to their 450th birthday celebrations. Director Trevor Nunn also revived the *Wars of the Roses* at the Rose Theatre, Kingston, in 2015, itself in commemoration of the 1964 RSC production.
25. Fay Davis, letter to the editor, *Birmingham Post*, 11 April 1951.
26. The Rep's theatre was on Station Street.
27. Ivor Brown, *Shakespeare Memorial Theatre 1951–53: A Photographic Record* (London: Max Reinhardt, 1953), 2.
28. Ibid., viii.
29. 'Foreword' to J. Dover Wilson and T. C. Worsley, *Shakespeare's Histories at Stratford, 1951* (New York: Theatre Arts Books, 1952), vii.
30. Ibid., 2–3.
31. Ibid., 5. Not all readers agree. In his 1817 *Characters of Shakespeare's Plays*, William Hazlitt argued that, if combined, the plays show Henry V as a faulty, insufficient national hero because the actions of Hal undermine those of Henry: the 'adventure on Gadshill was a prelude to the affair of Agincourt'. Reprinted in *The Romantics on Shakespeare*, ed. Bate, 164.

32. A similar rhetoric surrounds German cycles. Hortmann points out that amazement at the theatrical infrastructure was more memorable than the politics of Saladin Schmitt's 1927 ten-play cycle: 'Nobody doubted the massiveness of the achievement. For a middle-sized ensemble to possess seven actors able to play the different kings with equal competence shows the high level of training. It also extended to minor parts and extras who were all drilled to perfection'. But the politics 'left the critics guessing', so that 'the festival was its own justification' (Hortmann, 96).
33. Michael Billington, *State of the Nation: British Theatre since 1945* (London: Faber and Faber, 2007), 135.
34. I am particularly indebted to two histories of the RSC that cover these years in detail: Colin Chambers, *Inside the Royal Shakespeare Company* (New York: Routledge, 2004) and Sally Beauman, *The Royal Shakespeare Company: A History in Ten Decades* (Oxford: Oxford University Press, 1982).
35. Richard Pearson, *A Band of Arrogant and United Heroes: The Story of the Royal Shakespeare Company Production of the Wars of the Roses* (N.p.: Adelphi, 1991), ix.
36. Jack Tinker, review of 'The Plantagenets', directed by Adrian Noble, Royal Shakespeare Company, Barbican, London, *Daily Mail*, 11 April 1989.

Chapter 9
Afterword
The Seeds of Time

Graham Holderness

The grey eyes of the Time Traveller shone and twinkled, and his usually pale face was flushed and animated as he expounded his new theory. We sat in the garden of his house on Richmond Hill, under a huge clustering wisteria whose purple flowers dangled luxuriantly all around, sharing with us their brief moment of temporary perfection. The sun was setting over the tranquil Thames valley, and its dying rays touched with colour the bubbles that flashed and passed in our glasses. Cattle grazed contentedly in the broad meadow; the white sail of a yacht dipped and slewed along the shining river; and the bright air seemed hushed and suspended, as if time were standing still.

'Yes', he said, in conclusion. 'As I have explained, the machine I have designed is capable of carrying me to any point I choose, in space or in time'.

The three other guests had been introduced to me simply as the Artist, the Scientist and the Newspaper Man. The Time Traveller had lost none of his predilection for both stereotyping and anonymity.

'So using this machine', said the Artist, 'you can now go anywhere, anytime'.

'Theoretically, yes'.

'Then to where – and to when – do you plan to go?'

'That is exactly my purpose in inviting you gentlemen here this evening. My machine is not quite ready for its next expedition. I look to you to furnish me with suggestions as to whither I might travel. What should I attempt to see? To whom should I attempt to speak? Which time, and what place?'

'The Renaissance!' cried the Artist immediately. 'I would wish to see Michelangelo painting the ceiling of the Sistine Chapel'.

'Or to speak with Leonardo about his inventions', put in the Scientist. 'Find out how his mind really worked'.

'I would love to discover the true identity of the Mona Lisa!' said the Journalist. 'It would make my career'.

'All in good time', the Traveller laughed. 'For my first expedition I had not thought of travelling quite so far in space as Florence and Rome. Have you no interest in the history of your own country? Something a little closer, perhaps'.

'Then I would wish to witness Holbein painting the portrait of Henry VIII'.

'I would dearly love to speak to Sir Walter Raleigh, and learn the secrets of the School of Night'.

While the Journalist was still thinking of something to say, I could not forbear interrupting. 'I would wish to stand in the yard of the Globe Theatre on the first night of Shakespeare's *Hamlet*'.

'Shakespeare!' said the Time Traveller, as if the idea had never occurred to him. 'Why that would be interesting. I could ask him directly if he wrote his own plays! Do you think he would tell me?' The others laughed. 'But the age of Elizabeth was a remarkable period. And its history lies buried not more than a few miles from here'.

'Shakespeare', said the Artist in a voice of hushed veneration. 'Sweet Swan of Avon! To be able to return to that Golden Age, when our culture was still unspoiled by industry and commerce! Before the universal mechanization that has ruined our lives!'

'Balderdash!' cried the Scientist. 'The age of Elizabeth was the beginning of the modern age! Industry, manufacture, urbanization, transport, overseas trade, enclosure of the land – all had their origins there'.

'And yet Shakespeare's poetry breathes the breath of a cleaner age', returned the Artist. 'He dwelt in England's pleasant land, and knew nothing of our dark satanic mills'.

'Shakespeare was one of the first modern men', observed the Scientist, showing himself remarkably well-informed on the subject. 'He was a businessman and an entrepreneur. He formed one of the first joint-stock companies, composed of sharers in the theatre. He acquired an investment portfolio of property in Stratford and London. He supported land enclosure in Stratford, when most of his neighbours stood against it. His work was progressive and scientific. It has even been suggested that they were written by the foremost scientific philosopher of the day, Lord Bacon! If Shakespeare were alive today, do you think he would be mooning around Hammersmith looking for a boat to take him back to the Middle Ages? He would be our Poet Laureate, writing hymns to modernity and Progress'.

The Time Traveller seemed pleased with the energy of this debate. 'What is your opinion? He asked of me. 'I know you admire Shakespeare above all other writers'.

'I do', I said. 'And I have to agree with my friend the Artist, that his work comes to us from a very different world. A world of Nature rather than Science; where things were made by hand, not by machine; where men worked in the fields not in factories. I am no Luddite, but when I read Shakespeare, I cannot help feeling some nostalgia for the Forest of Arden, for Queen Mab, for the melodious magic of Midsummer's Eve. For the world we have lost. Shakespeare was not for an age, but for all time'.

'I see our friend is away with the fairies!' said the Scientist. 'Shakespeare was a man of the people. He wrote about human life in his own time, and his plays were performed for the entertainment and edification of those same people. He was the Charles Dickens of his day'.

'Why no', I broke in. 'There is no comparison. Shakespeare wrote for the court, for the Queen and the nobles. He was of the elite, not the masses. His patron was the Earl of Southampton. His company became the King's Men under James I. Popularity is irrelevant. His art survives because it was of the finest quality, not because of the number of copies he sold!'

'Gentlemen', said the Time Traveller, 'thank you all for your suggestions. I will endeavour to pursue them, if it is in any way possible. But now I must bid you good night, for I have some work to finish before I will be able to sleep. Come again tomorrow evening, all of you, to see me off'.

And so the party broke up. As hats and sticks were handed round, and goodbyes were being said in the hall, the Time Traveller signalled to me to linger behind the others. After they left, with a conspiratorial smile he led me back down the steps to the laboratory.

Ω

But let my narrative travel back in time a little, to explain the context of this conversation. I had rushed down to Richmond as soon as I heard of the Time Traveller's return. The last I had seen of him, three years before, was that momentary, fleeting glimpse of a transparent figure in the process of vanishing into futurity, that uncertain vision I tried to describe in my previous narrative. I had opened the laboratory door: there was a gust of air, a sound of breaking glass, and the Time Traveller was no longer there. The room was empty, save for a subsiding stir of dust.

I waited with wonder and anxiety for his return, imagining all the fates that might have befallen him on his long unpredictable voyage: whether he had perished under a blood-red, expiring sun, on some forlorn, apocalyptic shore; or found his true happiness among enlightened citizens of some utopian future. Imagine my feelings, then, when I received an invitation to dinner, signed with his own familiar hand, and delivered without comment, as if nothing had happened!

It was with mixed emotions, therefore, that I pushed open the gate of the house on Richmond Hill, one mild summer evening in 1903, and with no little trepidation, pulled at the doorbell. Almost throwing my hat and stick at the old manservant, I took the steps down to the laboratory two at time, and burst in on a familiar scene. There was the Time Traveller, his face as pale as I recalled it, his hair now as grey as his eyes, standing in front of what appeared to be a modified version of his Time Machine. He was in the midst of explaining its properties to three other guests, none of whom I knew. He greeted me cordially, but with a certain rueful air, as if knowing his unexplained absence merited some measure of contrition.

'How long have you been back?' I asked, muting my annoyance in deference to the presence of other guests.

'Oh, some while', he said offhandedly. 'I've had time for little but this'. And he gestured towards the Machine.

'So you say you have travelled in time', asked the Journalist, 'before, on such a machine?'

'Yes', said the Time Traveller, as if wanting to play down his previous adventures, 'but in a very experimental way. I wanted merely to prove that it could be done. There were many associated problems, and not a few risks. I had very little control over the machine's movements in space, and no means of storing it safely on my arrival. Why, at one point in my travels, I almost lost it altogether, which would have left me helplessly stranded in the future!'

The machine looked much the same to me, with what looked like some minor modifications. It had the same spherical structure of curved metal bars, the same intricate interconnection of rods and levers, fashioned from ivory and quartz. The saddle had been enlarged, and between the handlebars, the dials indicating the date seemed more elaborate. Above them I noted a new addition, a screen with what looked like a map of London.

The dinner-gong now resounded through the house, and we trooped upstairs and ate our meal quickly, in a silence of expectation.

'Let's talk outside', said the Time Traveller, and led us into his meticulously-kept garden, with splendid views of the valley of the Thames. Always the attentive host, the Time Traveller made sure all his guests were comfortable with brandy and cigars, before re-opening the conversation.

'What are your intentions, then', asked the Scientist, 'with this new machine?'

'So far, said the Time Traveller, carefully looking at the residue of ash on the end of his cigar, 'I have travelled only into the future. My ambition now is to journey into the past'.

'The past?' I exclaimed.

'Yes', said the Time Traveller, 'the past. If I can move through time in one direction, I can move in the other. In principle, the journey should entail less risk, since by definition we know more of the past than we do of the future. The problems are technical, rather than theoretical'.

'What are they?' asked the Journalist.

'They are physical. When I first ventured to travel into the future, I was particularly concerned with the interactions of time and space. Suppose my machine met with material obstacles in its temporal transit? My theory was that the velocity of time travel would attenuate the machine, so that I would slip like a vapour through the intervening substances. But to come to rest would involve jamming the machine and myself, molecule by molecule, into whatever lay in my way, and I had no idea what reaction that might cause. Might I not find myself inside a stone wall? In practice I found that time and space have some kind of intimate relationship with one another, such that I have coined a new term for its interdependence – space-time. Space-time has its own housekeeping rules, which do not permit two bodies to occupy the same physical space simultaneously. In whatever time I may happen to arrive in one particular place, space-time has already ensured the possibility of such an event, and thereby prohibited any destructive collision with another body. One day we will understand why. For the moment we can only be grateful for nature's providence.

'Now my original aspiration was to build a machine that would carry its operator indifferently in any direction of Space and Time. In practice I have moved only in Time, and did not attempt to navigate the other dimensions. Time travel was a blind, reckless, hurling of oneself into the void, and there was neither the opportunity nor the will to alter my position in space. But now I am confident that the speed of time travel eliminates the resistance of the material environment, I have no doubt that movement in space may also be accomplished'.

'But how can you navigate in space when abstracted from it by the mechanics of time travel?'

'A good question', he acknowledged. 'Yes, the Time Machine retains its materiality, although its molecules are reconfigured in flight. It is still subject to gravity, for instance, or the earth in its rotation would slip away from beneath it. But there is a way I do not yet fully understand of using Time to manoeuvre in Space. There are vectors in Time, just as the air has its currents, and using measurements taken from experiments in manned flight, I believe it possible to sail on them. The difficulty is knowing where you are! I have invented a device which uses electromagnetic waves to position an object in space. It transmits a signal to the nearest heavenly body – in our case the moon, of course – and receives it when it bounces back. The angle of incidence will tell me how far I have travelled from a fixed point, and in what direction. The result shows as a still or moving point on a map'. And he pointed to the screen at the front of the machine.

'Ingenious!' said the Scientist. 'A development of the Astrolabe'.

'Exactly so. And just as such instruments enabled our forefathers to discover new worlds on the other side of the globe, so mine will facilitate the exploration of time – and in due course, of Outer Space'.

It was then that he began to inquire of us as to what should be his destination.

Ω

And so it came about that once again I was standing in the Time Traveller's laboratory. The machine stood between us, quietly awaiting the signal that would send it rushing into the past.

'I really was concerned about you', I said, hurt by his prolonged absence incognito. 'I thought I would never see you again'.

'And I am truly sorry, my young friend,' was his reply, 'to have kept you in the dark. On the next occasion I will return to a point in time before I leave, and forewarn you of what is to come'.

'But where did you go?'

'Everywhere. This time I did not linger to have my machine stolen and my life attempted, but concentrated on studying the mechanics of time travel. I returned possessed of the key to many of its mysteries, and could think of nothing but applying my new knowledge to its practical problems. Only now am I fully equipped to travel again'.

'Now? But you said you were not yet ready'.

'An exaggeration. The machine is prepared. I wanted only some pointers as to where I should go. There is no point in organising a formal launch when I can easily return to the moment before it happened! No, my plan is to go tonight, and to return to the 17th century. Everything is ready'.

I looked ruefully at the machine. The thought that my companion would see the sun rise on Shakespeare's London filled me with envy. He looked at me and seemed to understand.

'I see you are anxious to find the solution to our controversy', he said. 'We certainly have enough questions to pursue. Was Shakespeare an Ancient, or a Modern? A conservative, or a radical? Did he write to bring back an old world, or to usher in a new? Did he write for the people, or the court? Did he stand for Art, or for Science?'

I confessed that I could wish for nothing more than to have the answers to such questions.

'Then', said the Time Traveller, quickly. 'Come with me'.

'With you?' I exclaimed. 'But ...'

'The machine can carry two. I constructed a pillion, as I thought I might need an assistant. Are you afraid?'

Of course I was, but I denied it. 'Now? Tonight?'

'Yes', he said, impatiently. 'We can return to this very moment, and afterwards you can go home and sleep in your own bed. But first, do you not want to meet Shakespeare?'

My resistance melted under his exhortations, and I resolved to travel with him. Immediately he bestrode the machine, and began to make adjustments to his dials.

'*Hamlet*, I think you said? That would be around 1600'.

'1603 was the year *Hamlet* was first published'.

'Very well. Observe how I can target our destination exactly, using my positioning system. The Globe Theatre. The southerly bank of the Thames, close to what is now the Iron Bridge. We are ready. Hop on!'

Wasting no more time, I slung a leg over the machine and sat behind him. He touched a lever, and we were off.

Ω

Although the Traveller had described in some detail the unpleasant sensations associated with travelling through Time, a helpless headlong motion, I was still unprepared for an experience that felt like nothing less than flinging oneself into a void. There was also, in addition, a violent buffeting of turbulence he had not mentioned in his previous narrative, that I assumed arose from the machine's simultaneous transit through space. I expected to observe the track of our passage in the changing landscape, but there was nothing to see in that grey, opaque limbo of non-existence, suspended between Space and Time. Suddenly, after only a few minutes, I felt the Time Traveller activate some instrument of deceleration, and the machine jolted to an abrupt stop.

We came to rest in the darkness, under a canopy of trees. Through their black branches I could glimpse moonlight, and not far off the yellow lights of a high-road.

'Where are we?' I asked, dismounting the machine. 'And when?'

'1851', he replied. 'Where, I'm not sure. We were travelling slightly off course and I had to stop to correct the deviation. I think we are in Hyde Park'.

He was bent over the machine trying to see his instruments, but by this time I had turned around, and was astonished at what I saw.

'Are you sure?' I asked.

'Yes', he said, 'no doubt. See, there is the Round Pond. And yonder is Kensington Palace'.

'No. About the date, I mean. If this is Hyde Park, what on earth is that?'

In the direction of the road, where I expected to see the spire of the Albert Memorial, I beheld a vast structure, surmounted by a great curved roof, apparently composed entirely of glass. It was larger than any building I had ever seen: well over a hundred feet in height and easily a third of a mile long. The bright moonlight reflected brilliantly from millions of panes of glass. I thought it must be some building of the future, and that the machine had borne us forwards, not backwards, in time.

'Why that' he exclaimed 'is a miracle of modern engineering. How could I have missed the significance? 1851! It is the Crystal Palace!'

'The Crystal Palace! Then we are in Sydenham?'

'No, no. The Crystal Palace was erected in Hyde Park for the Great Exhibition of 1851, and relocated later to Kent'.

'Can we take a closer look at it?'

'We can do more than that. We are only a few years back in time, in the age of our own parents. We will not excite attention: our clothes will seem little different from those of an ordinary working man. Before we resume our journey, we will be the first men to return from the future, and visit the Great Exhibition'.

'But what of the Time Machine? Where will you hide it?'

'Observe', he said, with that slightly mischievous air he assumed when about to demonstrate another of his inventions. From his pocket he drew what looked like a stop watch, set the dial, pointed it, and pressed a button. The machine trembled a little, grew faint and disappeared.

'What have you done?' I gasped.

'Have no fear', he said. 'I have sent the machine a few minutes into the future, where it will remain close, but utterly invisible to the present. When we wish to re-board, this remote control device will bring it back into our own time again'.

'Don't lose it!' I said fervently.

For a few hours of darkness we rested on a park bench, and at first light ventured into Kensington to find some breakfast. On the road we found the little green hut of the Cabman's Stand, where we were able to buy coffee and drink it in a dense atmosphere of thick smoke, frying onions and loud conversation. Then we returned to the park, and approached the Crystal Palace. As we walked past the ornamen-

pond with its fountains, the Time Traveller spoke reverently of the great building's history.

'You know he was a gardener, Paxton, designer of the Palace? A landscaper at Chatsworth. But he made use of new techniques in construction, combining wood, plate glass and cast iron, to design the great conservatory there. Have you seen the Chatsworth Lily House? Erected to house the *Amazonica*. A building with roof and walls of light. He used cast plate glass with a curtain wall system, so vertical bays of glass could be hung from cantilevered beams. That was his invention, and the basis for the construction of the Crystal Palace. Paxton said that the ribbed floating leaves of the giant Amazonian lily were his inspiration for this design. What a perfect marriage of art and nature! Of science and imagination!'

'Of architecture and engineering', I added, marvelling at the airy lightness of the huge building, and the delicacy of its crystalline structure.

'Yes. It must have been Brunel who saw its promise. You know he was on the selection committee that picked the design? In any event, he imitated the method, when he redesigned Paddington Station, and used the same construction company. Brunel now: he was a true visionary. A man of immense imagination, with the practical knowledge to realize his dreams'.

At the entrance the clerk looked curiously at our modern shillings, but allowed us in without comment. I believe he thought we were foreigners. We entered the building, and marvelled at both its structure and its contents. It was indeed a 'Great Exhibition of the Works of Industry of all Nations'. Everything was there, from countries all around the world, and from every discipline and field of art, manufacture, engineering, industry. There were jewels, and locks, and furniture, and daguerrotypes, and revolvers, and kitchen appliances, and sculptures, and cups, and barometers, and musical instruments. Ironwork from Shropshire, pots from Derby, a voting machine from Sussex, a reaping machine from America. Products from every new process, artefacts from every time and place. A Jacquard loom stood next to a statue of Anubis; here was a steam-hammer, there a gold howdah on a huge stuffed elephant.

'I think I see what I was looking for', said the Time Traveller, and threaded his way through the crowd that was gradually filling up the immense pavilion. He led me to a beautiful wrought-iron canopy standing right beneath the central dome of the Palace, which sheltered beneath its elaborate artistry a white plaster effigy of Shakespeare, copied from the statue in Westminster Abbey. The dome was a kind of cupola, fashioned from delicate traceries of wrought iron, exquisitely curved into an inverted flower-like shape. Slim iron columns supported the dome, each one surmounted by a perching eagle. At the apex a cylindrical chimney tapered into a kind of spire, topped by a weather-vane and a figure of Eros. Somehow the heavy iron structure managed to assume an effect of lightness, the iron seeming as fragile as lace, and easily mistaken for a garden trellis threaded with clambering flowers.

'The dome is from Coalbrookdale', said the Time Traveller. 'You know the scientific history, of course: how Abraham Darby made advances in the smelting of iron, using coke as fuel. How his company built the first iron bridge. This work of theirs takes pride of place here: a perfect synthesis of beauty and industry, of art and manufacture'.

I could hardly not be impressed by this interweaving of art and industry, metallurgy and imagination. 'It reminds me of the Eiffel Tower', I exclaimed. 'The same latticework of iron, the same organic form'.

A gentleman who was making a close study of the canopy looked at me curiously.

'Keep your voice down', whispered the Time Traveller. 'Remember we're in 1851! Let us hope that man lives another fifty years, so he can see the Eiffel Tower for himself. It will surprise him to remember when he first heard about it. But here, at any rate, is one image of Shakespeare for you, at the very centre of the exhibition your hero William Morris refused to enter! Does he not look entirely at home?'

I owned that he did, and that here in this miraculous glass palace, modelled on the leaves of a lily; constructed by means of the most advanced engineering technology; at the heart of a Great Exhibition that gave equal emphasis to art and industry – the figure of Shakespeare seemed in no way out of place. By now a crowd had gathered, and we were able to observe the diverse and colourful throng of spectators that gathered and circled around the monument's base. A gentleman in top-hat, mutton-chop whiskers, frock coat and white trousers, the very image of Victorian respectability, was explaining its form to two men from Persia, dressed in brilliant red, blue and yellow costumes, with baggy trousers and white turbans. There was a man in blue naval officer's uniform with gold-braided cocked hat, his bonneted wife on his arm. Two little girls in frocks sat casually at the monument's base, poring over a printed catalogue. The elaborate flowered costumes and coolie hats of imperial China complemented the flowing robes and turbans of India. A stout Englishman in brown broadcloth and gaiters stood and stared at the monument with the ingrained truculence of a farmer.

This colourful and cosmopolitan throng skirted the frontal base of the statue. We walked around the back, and were there confronted by a very different scene. Here a large group of common people stood and sat around, completely at their leisure beneath the Bard's avuncular gaze. A red-faced woman, basket at her feet, held out a glass to be filled with wine by an equally rubicund man. Two soldiers in shakos flirted loudly with a couple of pretty country girls. There were children everywhere: a small boy with his father's hand-me-down hat slipping over his ears; a little girl holding wool for her busily knitting mother; and at the centre of the pedestal, a nursing mother suckled her baby at her breast, her own mother looking indulgently on.

'All human life is here', said the Time Traveller, 'gathered together under Shakespeare's masterful shadow'.

'"One touch of nature"', I quoted, '"makes the whole world kin"'.

'Indeed. And there is the answer to one of our questions, at least for this time and for this place. There is no separation here between Shakespeare and the common people. Moreover, they themselves are enfolded within a cosmopolitan gathering of all nations, the focal point of which is the image of Shakespeare. Your quotation is very apt. But do you know what Prince Albert said was the ultimate purpose of the Great Exhibition? To bring closer "that great end, to which all history points – the realisation of the unity of mankind"'.

As the place gradually began to fill with more and more visitors, we thought it best to make our exit. It was a short walk across the park to the clump of trees where we had left the Time Machine. He pressed a button on his remote control, and the machine materialized out of thin air a few yards away.

'We will stop here again on the way back', he said, adjusting his instruments. 'There is more to be seen. The device will memorise this exact point in space and time, like a grid reference on a map'.

People turned to look at us, but showed little curiosity, imagining the machine, I suppose, to be yet another ingenious invention from the technological cornucopia of the Great Exhibition. In any case we were aboard and away in a matter of seconds.

Again there was that sensation of dropping like a stone into the vortex of time, and the violent clubbing force of space pushing us back on track. On this occasion the Time Traveller seemed confident of his navigation, and we held our course for what seemed like a long duration. As we began to decelerate, I could see the years receding more slowly on the spinning dials, counting down to our target date of 1603.

And we were there. I almost leapt from the machine, in eagerness to enter this so hallowed and so gracious time. The Time Traveller reset his dials back to 1851 again, and alighted. Preparing to cache the machine into the future, he turned and looked around. What we both saw gave us pause, and immediately suspended our aspirations to dwell for very long in Shakespeare's London.

Ω

We stood on the bank of the river, surrounded by all those famous historical monuments so carefully chronicled in the engravings of Visscher and Hollar: London Bridge, the old St Paul's, and the Globe Theatre itself, standing squat and round next to the bear-baiting arena. But something was out of joint. The waters of the Thames ran sluggish and grey, its surface covered in floating debris. There was a strange ominous hush. Not a soul was abroad, though the morning was well advanced. Everywhere a sweet sickly smell clung to everything, an odour of decay. Beyond the thatched roofs of the clustering houses, plumes of smoke from bonfires smudged the horizon. From an open window there came the thin cry of a new-born child. Otherwise there was no sound of a human presence. A scattering of white dust hung limply in the air.

Instinctively we stuck close to the machine, afraid of this inhospitable environment. The doors of the theatre frowned shut. Nearby an indescribably filthy old man was rummaging through a pile of rubbish.

'Good day', I greeted him.

He snarled at me like a wild animal disturbed over its prey, then looked us up and down with contempt. 'Foreigners', he spat.

'Is the theatre open?'

'Theatre's closed'.

'Why?'

He looked at me, and began to laugh softly. 'Why?' he repeated.

'Yes, why?'

He opened a mouth full of carious teeth. 'Plague'.

We had unwittingly chosen a bad year to revisit Jacobean London, and I wished I had thought more carefully when asked to choose a date. Immediately we climbed back on the machine. Not only would we have no resistance to the dreadful bubonic bacillus: worse, we could contract the disease, and return to our own time as carriers of a devastating infection. The old man stared at us without curiosity. After all he had seen, I imagine it would have been no surprise to him to behold Ezekiel's chariot, riding the whirlwind through that smitten, pestilential city.

Ω

We made haste to leave that dreadful place behind us. As the Traveller started the machine, I noticed him accidentally nudge one of the dials controlling the date, changing the '8' to a '9'. But it was too late to warn him, and we were away. With no spatial relocation, time travel was almost tolerable. The Traveller seemed not to notice the altered date, and we had soon overshot our target. But as we approached 1951, we became aware of some cataclysmic activity in the space-time continuum. Dull percussions reached us, attenuated but cacophonous, as if a massive devastating force were obliterating the world outside. I feared we might become victims of some apocalyptic event, but the noise of destruction soon ceased, and we coasted easily enough to our destination, and touched down gently in 1951.

I explained to my companion how the error of timing had occurred. Apprehensively we looked around, but the world seemed peaceful enough, though recently ravaged by a terrible disaster. Along the banks of the Thames we saw the marks of devastation, ruined buildings, piles of rubble.

'What caused this', I wondered. 'Earthquake?'

'No', said the Time Traveller thoughtfully. 'I think not. I foresaw something very like this, and wrote a paper on it. I believe this is the result of war from the air. Of aerial bombardment. The city has endured terrible punishment from a ruthless enemy, equipped with weapons of mass destruction'.

Still the marks of devastation were perhaps not so recent: flourishing vegetation sprang and clustered among the ruins, and everywhere we could see signs of clearance and reconstruction. We hid the machine, and walked upstream towards Westminster. Across the Thames, the dome of St Paul's still stood proudly, though its neighbourhood was in ruins. We walked beneath the Charing Cross railway bridge, and my companion pointed out the old brick piles preserved from Brunel's original structure.

'Brunel again', he said. 'Is there no escape from that man's genius?'

The old Strand Bridge had obviously been recently replaced by a new structure, apparently now known as Waterloo Bridge. As we walked towards Westminster Bridge, we began to realize that something unusual was taking place here. Crowds of people in holiday mood were converging on the south bank of the river, and everywhere pennants and bunting, brightly-coloured posters and hoardings, heralded some great celebration or festival. It did not take us long to realize that, by a fortuitous error of navigation, we had stumbled upon the first anniversary of the Great Exhibition, and that its name was the Festival of Britain.

As we rounded the bend of the river, we were confronted by a breathtaking collection of buildings, some temporary and some permanent, evidently erected for the festival. One in particular stood out as an extraordinary construction in a modern, Scandinavian style, a great concert hall with a tall glazed facade and a curved roof, its name emblazoned on the front as the 'Royal Festival Hall'. A high and slender shape, the 'Skylon', somewhere between a cigar and a rocket, hung suspended in the air with no visible means of support. Other buildings included an enormous dome, in the shape artists have imagined to belong to alien spacecraft, and a very tall vertical barn-like building with a timber trussed roof of oak that swept and curved upwards at the sides, and a façade all of glass, named 'the Lion and the Unicorn'. Threading our way through the crowds, we wandered into this latter building, which was an exhibition space telling the story of the British people. A large mural depicted scenes from British history, and the exhibition itself documented the history of our institutions, parliament and the law and the church. We were pleased to find, in pride of place, a copy of the First Folio of Shakespeare's works, alongside a King James Bible.

This positioning of Shakespeare as part of the constitutional history of Britain seemed, however, somewhat conventional, and there was little interest in it from the crowds of visitors who streamed through the building.

'Perhaps our Shakespeare is no longer at the heart of the British character', suggested the Time Traveller, 'if he is only a book among books'.

We exited the building, and walked over to a spot where a crowd of people were gathered, staring up at a steam locomotive that stood on display beneath a temporary covering. The engine was in many ways little different from the trains we knew, but it was much more beautifully designed, with clean lines and a stylish finish. The wheels were more discreet, half-concealed inside the bodywork, while the tall chimney stack we were used to had been flattened to give the locomotive a smooth, aerodynamic look. It was painted a bright green, with a black front that bore a green shield decorated with the words 'Golden Arrow', and below a bright red bumper. An actual golden arrow slanted diagonally across the shield in what seemed to us a very avant-garde, asymmetrical gesture. Altogether the machine was a beautiful piece of design engineering, sleek and classic in its lines, bright and modern in its decoration, exuding a quiet and confident sense of power. It was basically the same machine, the steam locomotive invented by Stephenson over a century before, yet in terms of craftsmanship, design quality and engineering precision it seemed to us miraculous.

But a surprise lay in store for us, as we moved around with the admiring crowd. We observed that some of them were pointing up at a red name-plate, riveted to the side of the locomotive, and laughing with pleasure amongst themselves. Peering over their heads to see what was stimulating them, we realized that we had once again stumbled upon the object of our quest. The locomotive was named 'William Shakespeare'.

'"Britannia Class no. 70004, William Shakespeare"', the Traveller read from an expository placard. 'So here he is again, back where he belongs, at the centre of public attention. And at the cutting edge of modern technology and design'.

Ω

At last we felt it was time to be on our way. We returned to the spot where we had left the machine, full of admiration for the evidence we had seen of British scientific and technological development, especially after years of a cruel and destructive war; and delighted to have found proof that Shakespeare remained not only central to British culture, but intimately bound up with the principal social and economic drivers of the day, industry, engineering and design. My curiosity about the future was only increased by our sojourn in 1951, so I was delighted when the Time Traveller indicated a willingness to attempt one more progressive cycle.

'Why don't we go further forward, and see if Shakespeare figures as largely in the second anniversary of the Great Exhibition?' he said. 'Have a look at Shakespeare 2051?'

I agreed with alacrity, and he set his dials for that date. I had another idea. 'Suppose we shift our physical location, and visit Shakespeare's birthplace, Stratford-on-Avon, in 2051? It will be interesting to see what has happened to the old town'.

No sooner said than done. The Traveller used a kind of keyboard fitted to his map to enter the place-name 'Stratford', and once again we committed ourselves to a journey through time and space. After a brief period of motion, involving some little relocation, the machine seemed to slow itself down, as if reluctant to proceed any further. The dials showed that we were past the second millennium, but there seemed to be some obstacle inhibiting us from voyaging any further than 2012. The machine stopped in that year, in a clump of trees by a river. The Traveller sat staring at his instruments, and scratching his head.

'I don't understand', he said. 'Something is preventing us from proceeding further. The continuum seems to end here. We seem to be locked inside a paradigm, and have reached its outer limit. It is almost as if we are caught in a temporal narrative that is only being written at this time, and has no perspective on the future'.

'But we have been travelling into the future', I said.

'Our tomorrow', he retorted, 'but someone else's yesterday. The machine cannot see beyond 2012, and so we are held here, like characters imprisoned in an author's past'.

'An author? But who is writing the story?'

'I don't know. I've never believed in God. And where are we? The map shows we've travelled only a few miles north-east. I don't think we're in Stratford-upon-Avon'.

That much was obvious, as we peered out from our hiding place. The light was fading towards dusk. We stood in a small wooded riverside area, hidden from view, so no-one had witnessed our arrival. But this was no more than a little landscaped seclusion, part of a much larger public space that was a concourse for literally thousands of people. We were in an enormous park, full of huge buildings, seemingly constructed for sporting events. Prominent among them was an immense stadium, tall and circular, engineered with outstanding ingenuity, and exquisitely designed. Gradually, as darkness began to fall, innumerable coloured lights, set into intricate patterns, began to illuminate the structure, forming varying patterns and shapes, so what had been a large building turned into a fantasy palace of glowing vermilion. We had never seen so much power, generated presumably from electricity, and applied to such subtle and aesthetically thrilling purposes.

We hid the machine, and walked towards the stadium. After a few brief observations, the Time Traveller said: 'I know where we are. We should have given the machine more precise instruction. This is Stratford in London's East End!'

I was concerned that we would be detected, since the fashions of clothing had changed enormously, and we stood out in our anachronistic dress. But as we approached the building, suddenly we found ourselves part of a large throng of people, all dressed in various fashions of the past, from the Middle Ages up to our own time. We were able to fall in with a group of men, clad in authentic 19th century costume, who seemed to be on their way to a game of cricket. Filing along with them, we remained unnoticed, and were thus able to gain access to the interior of the stadium.

Once inside, our astonishment only increased. The stadium was a huge arena, with raked seating holding what looked like 100,000 people. The round competition or performance space was filled with what appeared to be a landscaped area of bright green grass, at its centre a mound or tumulus surmounted by an oak tree. The lighting inside the arena was even more brilliant and impressive than its exterior illumination. We soon realised that our costumed companions must in fact be actors in a show about to commence, so as they approached the stage we stepped aside, and ensconced ourselves in two empty seats at the rear of the auditorium.

As we seated ourselves, we heard the announcement that told us where we were: the venue of the 30th Olympic Games. We had known only two Olympiads, of course, in Athens in 1896 and Paris in 1900. Evidently the custom had been continued every four years ever since. This was the opening ceremony. The show that unfolded before us, involving hundreds of actors and as many musicians, was nothing less than a history of Britain. The bright green sward, with its towering mound that bore a resemblance to Glastonbury Tor, represented mediaeval England, a pre-industrial landscape of fields and villages, meadows and woods. Smoke rose from the chimney of a thatched cottage. Actors playing the roles of rural labourers tilled the fields or played games, kicking a ball or dancing round a maypole. Our friends the cricketers, who had helped us to enter incognito, played their game with impressive earnestness on the village green. All the while a sweet child's voice sang William Blake's poem 'And did those feet' from *Jerusalem,* a nostalgic celebration of England's green and pleasant land, as yet unblighted by the dark satanic mills.

It was difficult to comprehend everything being played before us, as the arena was so vast, and we were surrounded by an immense battery of lights, and a great wall of sound, voices and music, the source of which we could not identify. Huge screens projected above the rim of the arena, showing what appeared to be gigantic moving photographs of distant scenes. But presently some significant historical change was foreshadowed, when an old omnibus drawn by two shire horses entered the arena, and deposited a group of men who wore the top hats and frock coats of Victorian capitalists. One of them, who seemed to be *primus inter pares*, strode ahead of the group, carrying a book. We realised immediately that this actor was representing none other than Isambard Kingdom Brunel himself. But to our surprise, he stood on the mound, and in a ringing declamatory voice spoke Caliban's lines from *The Tempest*:

> Be not afeard. The isle is full of noises,
> Sounds and sweet airs that give delight and hurt not.
> Sometimes a thousand twangling instruments
> Will hum about mine ears, and sometime voices
> That, if I then had waked after long sleep,
> Will make me sleep again; and then, in dreaming,
> The clouds methought would open, and show riches
> Ready to drop upon me, that when I waked,
> I cried to dream again.

As he spoke, splendidly from that unseen source rose music, grand and melancholy, growing in crescendo to a paean that filled the arena. But this was no modern music, but an anthem from our own time! We recognised it instantly as Elgar's 'Nimrod', which I had myself heard premiered at St James's Hall in 1899. Evidently the music of our own day was not only still popular, but regarded as a quintessential *leitmotif* of the British sensibility.

There followed an extraordinary performed history of the Industrial Revolution. The rural populace began to drift away, while by some invisible technology the great oak tree on the summit of the mound rose into the air, revealing beneath its roots a pit emitting smoke and light. From this breach in the rural landscape there began to stream myriads of industrial workers, ragged with poverty and dirty with toil. Under the beneficent gaze of Brunel and his band of entrepreneurs, the working masses occupied the arena, beginning to roll up the green carpet of grass, and remove it to disclose hard surfaces of metal or glass. Fences were planted to represent land enclosure. Women and men were seen hauling laboriously at machines that somehow, to our astonishment, triggered from the ground tall factory chimneys, six in number, that rose into the air and belched forth the smoke and steam of industrial production. Brunel strode cheerfully though the midst of this immense social upheaval, surveying the apparently infinite capability of human labour.

By now the green grass of rural England had disappeared, replaced by a brownfield industrial site full of machinery: a water wheel, beam engines, looms. And then came the most incredible theatrical manifestation I had ever seen. At the centre of the display I had noticed a large circular trough, linked by a long channel to a crucible that put me in mind of steel production. Now before our very eyes that same smelting process seemed to begin, with what looked like a sparking river of molten steel pouring into the channel, and slowly making its way towards the central trough. Steelworkers busily hammered and sieved the glowing ore. In truth the display was manufactured by a combination of light effects and fireworks; but no more convincing simulation of smelting has, I am sure, ever before or since been done on a stage. Running around the trough, the molten steel appeared to form a perfect ring. Above our heads, we noticed, four identical rings of light were hovering suspended in the air, slowly converging towards one another. The ring that had shaped itself in the centre also rose and moved towards the others. In a dazzling technological *coup d'oeil*, these five rings, that seemed to have the mass and density of metal, yet hovered ethereally in the air, effortlessly combined together to form an image, which then seemed to burst into flame, and cascade showers of brilliant sparks down into the space of the auditorium.

'The symbol of the Olympics', said the Time Traveller, gazing up with something like awe at the interlacing rings. 'Pierre de Coubertin showed me his design. Derived from an ancient Greek heiroglyph. All the nations of the world, linked together in peaceful competition. It is wonderful'.

'Man has a bright future, then, at least for a hundred years or so'.

'And one in which our own time is remembered and revered. The hero of this show is none other than Brunel!'

'Yet the only words he spoke were from Shakespeare'.

'Yes. What do you make of that?'

A pretty young girl in a seat next to the Time Traveller overheard his question and said helpfully 'It's from *The Tempest*. We did it at school'.

Like many other members of the audience, the girl held in her hand a small oblong machine that clearly interested the Time Traveller. I had observed her entering writing onto a screen, as if sending messages. Now however she pressed her fingers onto the device, and conjured up for us on the screen a tiny image of the actor playing Brunel, speaking Shakespeare's lines.

'May I?' asked the Time Traveller, and took the device from her hand. 'Lumiere would be interested to see this', he said thoughtfully.

'You can keep it', said the girl. 'It's only a Pay-as-you-go. I've got a contract phone'.

'I'm sure you have', he said, concealing his incomprehension. But I saw him slide the device quickly into his pocket, before she changed her mind. I noticed two ushers pointing at us, and talking to one another. We both felt it was time for us to move on, though the show was continuing. We slipped out the way we had come in, and returned to the spot where we had left the Time Machine.

'Why do you think they used those lines of Shakespeare?' My companion asked as we walked. 'From Caliban to Brunel? Brunel was no dreamer, and certainly no primitive man'.

'I've been reflecting on it', I replied, 'and think I have the answer. We have just witnessed the same creative conjunction of Shakespeare with industry and engineering that we saw in the Great Exhibition, and in the Festival of Britain. Caliban lived in a wondrous isle, surrounded by the shapes of his imagination. He was an instinctive artist, a poet and a dreamer. He heard random noise as exquisite music, and when he looked at the sky, he saw the clouds open onto infinite possibility.

'Brunel too lived in an isle of wonders, and heard the same music. He listened to the random babbling of nature, and interpreted it into a common language. He dreamed the same dreams: dreams of space and time. And what he dreamed, he invented: his mind and hand went together. His imagination reached out across distance, abbreviated time and annihilated space, crossed rivers and linked towns, burrowed deep into the earth, and rode the pitching waves of the high seas. And from those visions, he conjured machines that made dreams into reality: bridges, ships, railways.

'This we knew already. But what we have seen here tonight, takes Brunel's machinery, and renders it back into dream again. The technology of 2012 far surpasses that of our own day, and is capable not only of construction, but of creation. Engineering has entered the realm of poetry. Art and science have become one, as they were in the Renaissance. And so Shakespeare and Brunel no longer stand opposed, as the dreamer and the artisan, or the poet and the engineer. They have become one voice, one hand, one mind. And by the combination of their powers of vision and practice, they have kept Britain great, or perhaps made it great again'.

Ω

We retrieved the machine, and prepared to bid farewell to the future, and return to the past. I thought we would be going straight home, but the Time Traveller was thoughtful, studying the device the girl had given him.

'Let's have one more try at finding Shakespeare', he said quickly. 'I'd like to show him this. So he can see how his words will live on in the future'.

And we were away again. Accustomed by now to time travel, its sensations had become tolerable. The Traveller has obviously perfected his directional instruments, and steered the machine confidently back to Southwark, this time to the less perilous date of 1599, and a time around late morning. Elizabethan London now seemed a much more normal place, with the sun breaking through clouds, early risers going about their business, and the river gliding at its own sweet will. Smoke rose from chimneys, sounds of children and smells of cooking came from open windows. We hid the machine, and asked at the door of the theatre if there was to be a play that day. The answer was unfortunately negative, so we inquired into the whereabouts of Master William Shakespeare. We would find him, we were told, later in the day, along the river at the George and Dragon Inn.

So we walked along to the old high street, our clothes courting curious glances, but no interference, as the district was a favourite haunt of foreigners. We found the old inn easily enough – it remains there still – and entered its grey cobbled yard. Inside we were able to purchase food and drink with a small silver coin I happened to find in my pocket. A few rough-looking characters eyed us, but gave us no trouble. We waited, and as the hours passed, people came and went, workers, servants, apprentices, gentlemen, soldiers, players, prostitutes, taking a drink and going about their business. We sat watching in fascination the colourful pageant of Shakespeare's London. Before our very eyes appeared the contemporary originals of Shakespeare's dramatic characters: that angry young man had a touch of Hotspur; the lean and slippered pantaloon resembled Justice Shallow; there was Doll Tearsheet, and around her a whole crowd of fat, red-faced and boisterous Falstaffs.

But Shakespeare himself never appeared. The little communications device the Traveller had brought back from the future seemed to stop working, its display showing a warning of 'no signal'. We had lost our link to the future, and no-one was expecting us in the past. As the light began to fail we gave up, and returned to the Time Machine. Silently, not without a tinge of disappointment, we recovered the machine, re-boarded and returned to our own time.

Ω

Everything was as we had left it. The laboratory remained silent and undisturbed. The clock on the wall told us that no time at all had elapsed since we embarked on that incredible journey.

'If you hurry, you'll still catch the last train', he said to me in a strangely matter-of-fact way. 'But come tomorrow night, won't you, to help me convince the others that I'm neither mad, nor an inveterate liar!'

As I walked towards the station, down the hill into the little town, quotidian reality encroached and pressed upon me, claiming me for this time, and this place. The hissing of gas lamps along the street; low laughter of lovers in the nearby park; the distant sigh of a train from over the hill, making its way to Kingston. Yet in my mind, all this was fractured and transected by an unavoidable awareness of other times, and other places; of lives long gone, yet still inexplicably present; of ages still unknown, yet into which, against all laws of nature, I had already travelled. All our yesterdays remaining to be revisited; tomorrow as easily accessible as today. Was I here, or there, or elsewhere? Did those street-lamps illuminate a flare-path to the future? Was that whispering I could hear from over the low wall, a lover and his lass, an echo from the past? Would my train really take me only a few miles away in space, back to a humdrum, imprisoning present?

Be not afeard, I said to myself. The isle is full of noises. Everything is still there, if our dreams are true enough: all that is past, and passing, and to come. I had no idea whether I was still dreaming, or had wakened from long sleep. Or perhaps there was little difference between the two. In any event, as I walked briskly through Richmond, Caliban's rich imagination and inconsolable longing burned within me; and though I was far from unhappy, I cried to dream again.

Graham Holderness is the author or editor of some 60 books. His work can be divided into three strands: literary criticism, theory and scholarship, especially in Shakespeare studies; the pioneering of an innovative new method of 'creative criticism'; and creative writing in fiction, poetry and drama. Key critical works include *The Shakespeare Myth* (Manchester UP, 1988), *The Politics of Theatre and Drama* (Routledge, 1992), *Shakespeare: The Histories* (Bloomsbury, 2000), and *The Faith of William Shakespeare* (Lion Books, 2016). Works of creative criticism, which are half criticism and half fiction, include *Nine Lives of William Shakespeare* (Bloomsbury-Arden Shakespeare, 2011); *Tales from Shakespeare: Creative Collisions* (Cambridge University Press, 2014) and *Re-writing Jesus: Christ in 20th Century Fiction and Film* (Bloomsbury, November 2014). He has also published two novels: *The Prince of Denmark* (University of Hertfordshire Press, 2001), and the historical fantasy novel *Black and Deep Desires: William Shakespeare Vampire Hunter* (Top Hat Books, 2015).

Index

NOTE: *Page references with an f are figures; page references with an n will be found in Notes.*

A

Adams, Thomas, 25n9
African Americans, tercentenary celebrations (1916) and, 85–86, 91n45
Albert (Prince), 133
Aldermanbury monument. *See* First Folio monument, Aldermanbury
Anderson, Benedict, 2
Anne Hudgins Shakespeare Class, domestic practices in, 72–73
Antony and Cleopatra (Shakespeare), 63n34
Arte of English Poesie, The (Puttenham), 16
As You Like It (Shakespeare), 36, 98
authorship controversy, 44

B

Bacon, Francis, 44
Barnard, John, 99
Bennett, Susan, 66
Berlioz, Hector, 7
Binyon, Laurence, 51
Birmingham Repertory Theatre (Rep), 109–10, 112–15
Blake, William, 140
Book of Homage (1916) (Gollancz), 6, 11n16, 93–95, 100
Borges, Jorge Luis, 27–28, 37
Brown, Ivor, 114
Brunel, Isambard Kingdom, 9, 131, 136, 141–44
Burns, Robert, 8

C

Calderón, Pedro, de la Barca, 8
Caliban by the Yellow Sands (MacKaye), 5, 79, 86
Carlyle, Thomas, 8
Cartelli, Thomas, 78–79
Casson, Hugh, 58, 60
Cavendish, Sir Charles, 16
Celtdom, 94, 97
Cervantes, Miguel de, 8
Channel Tunnel, inauguration of (1994), 4
Chaplin, Martin, 58
churches, ruined, 63n36
   as war memorials, 46–48, 51–60, 63n45
Churchill, Winston, 52–53, 59
class, 123–24, 133
   tercentenary celebrations (1916) and, 85
Coleridge, Samuel Taylor, 110
collective memory, 2, 23
   women's clubs and, 74–75
commemoration. *See* specific topics
commemorative events
   Book of Homage (1916) as, 93–95
   at Channel Tunnel, inauguration of (1994), 4
   cycle performances as, 108–17, 118n5, 118n7, 119n31, 120n32
   at Festival of Britain (1951), 3–4, 109–17, 119n19, 136–38

First Folio (1623) as, 4–5, 49–50
First Folio monument (1896)
    as, 4, 41–45, 49–60, 61n4,
    62n13, 62nn28–29, 63n34
at Great Exhibition (1851), 4, 8–
    9, 109, 129–33, 136
Great Shakespeare Jubilee
    (1769), 3, 8, 28–31, 38n25,
    38n27, 39n48
at London Olympics (2012), 9,
    140–44
Royal Gala (1830), 3, 28, 32–36,
    39n48, 39n53
tercentenary celebration (1864),
    36, 38n16, 39n72
women's clubs and, 5, 65–75
. *See also* tercentenary celebrations (1916)
commendatory poems in First Folio, 57
community drama, 86, 92n49
Condell, Henry, 28, 41–60, 61n3, 61n6,
    62n27
. *See also* First Folio; First Folio
    monument, Aldermanbury
Connell, Charles, 61n7
Connerton, Paul
    rituals of commemoration and,
        30–32, 35, 74, 77n56
    social memory and, 77n54
cooking, women's clubs and, 71–72
cosmopolitanism, 133
Coubertin, Pierre de, 142
Crystal Palace at Great Exhibition of
    1851, 129–31, 136
Cust, Lionel, 94
cycle performances
    as event theatre, 115, 117
    Festival of Britain and, 109–17
    First Folio and, 110
    German, 108, 111, 120n32
    of Histories, 108–17, 118n5,
        118n7, 119n31
    indispensable unstageability
        and, 115–17
    national identity, British, and,
        109–12, 115–16
    origins of, 109–10
    Rep and, 109–10, 112–15
    SMT and, 109, 112–16

'Wars of the Roses' cycle, RSC,
    as, 108–9, 116–17, 118n5
Cymbeline (Shakespeare), 25n9

D

Dallas Shakespeare Club, First Folio
    purchased by, 69
Dante Alighieri, 8, 59
Dávidházi, Péter, 29
da Vinci, Leonardo, 122
Davis, Fay, 113
Death of the Statues, 6–8
De la Fontaine, Jean, 7
Deutsche Shakespeare-Gesellschaft
    (German Shakespeare Society), 3, 4
Devil's banket described in four sermons (Adams), 25n9
Digges, Leonard, 4
Dingelstedt, Franz von, 108–9
Dobson, Michael, 36
domestic commemorations by
    women's clubs, 71–75
Dover Wilson, John, 115
Draaisma, Douwe, 70
Drama League of America, 91n31
    tercentenary celebrations (1916)
        and, 83
dramatic procession, Royal Gala of
    1830 and, 32–34

E

'East Coker' (Eliot), 58
Eiffel Tower, 132
Elgar, Edward, 141
Eliot, T. S., 47, 53, 60
Elizabeth, age of
    modernity of, 122–23
    plague and, 134
embodied epitaphs, 14–15, 19
    Thomas Nashe on, 17–18
epitaphs
    as commands, 16–22
    corpses serving as, 22–23
    embodied, 14–15, 17–19
    in first person, 13
    Hamlet and, 14
    Henry V and, 18–19, 22–23
    Henry VI and, 17, 20–22
    Histories and, 1–2, 15
    as identifying corpse, 20

Richard II and, 17
    sermons and, 25n9
Esty, Jed, 111
European Shakespeare Research Association (ESRA), 4–5
event theatre, cycle performances as, 115, 117

F

Festival of Britain (1951), 9, 119n19
    cycle performances and, 109–17
    First Folio and, 137
    Histories and, 3–4
    Royal Festival Hall and, 136–37
    William Shakespeare locomotive at, 137–38
First Folio (1623), 4–5
    commendatory poems in, 57
    cycle performances and, 110
    Festival of Britain and, 137
    Shakespeare reconstructed by, 49–51
    Tercentenary of, 11n14
    women's club purchasing, 69
First Folio monument, Aldermanbury (1896), 4, 61n4, 62n13
    First Folio book displayed in, 49
    First Folio extracts on, 42–43
    installation of, 41–42
    patronage and, 42
    Plaque 1 of, 43
    Plaque 2 of, 42–43
    Plaque 3 of, 42, 45
    Plaque 4 of, 43
    as tombstone, 45
    Walker and, 43–45, 49, 53–54, 58–59, 62nn28–29, 63n34
    as war memorial, 45, 51–60
Flint, Kate, 71
Flower, Charles, 36
forgetting
    Henry V and, 2, 23–24
    Much Ado About Nothing and, 2
Fournier, Paul, 7
Foxe, John, 59
Frayn, Michael, 119n19
Fussell, Paul, 95

G

Garrick, David, 3, 38n7
    . *See also* Great Shakespeare Jubilee (1769)
Georgia, tercentenary celebrations (1916) in, 80, 84–86
Germany, cycle performances in, 108, 111, 120n32
Giles, Judy, 72–73
Globe, Shakespeare's (London), 119n24
Goethe, Johann Wolfgang, 8
Gollancz, Israel, 93–95
Gounaridou, Kiki, 110
Gower Monument (Stratford-upon-Avon), 6
Great Exhibition (1851), 4, 8, 109, 132–33
    Brunel and, 131, 136
    Crystal Palace, at, 129–31, 136
Great Shakespeare Jubilee (1769), 3, 8, 38n27, 39n48
    impetus for, 28–29
    masquerade ball in, 31
    plays performed at, 38n25
    unifying purpose of, 30
The Great War and Modern Memory (Fussell), 95
Ground Zero, excavation of, 56

H

Halbwachs, Maurice, 74
Hall, Peter, 116–17
Hamlet (Shakespeare), 1, 128–29
    epitaphs in, 14
Hampton-Reeves, Stuart, 110–12
Handel, Georg Friedrich, 8
Hardy, Thomas, 55
Hauer, Christian E., Jr., 48, 63n36
Hawkes, Terence, 100
Hazlitt, William, 119n31
Heminge, John, 28, 41–60, 61n3, 61n6, 62n27
    . *See also* First Folio; First Folio monument, Aldermanbury
Henderson, Diana, 103
Henry IV (Shakespeare), 25n9
Henry V (Shakespeare)
    epitaphs in, 18–19, 22–23

forgetting in, 2, 23–24
Jones and, 6, 95–104
national identity, British, and, 93–94, 100
Henry VI (Shakespeare), 119n24
epitaphs in, 17, 20–22
as monumental play, 107–17
national identity, British and, 112–13
Histories (Shakespeare)
cycle performances of, 108–17, 118n5, 118n7, 119n31
epitaphs in, 1–2, 15
Festival of Britain and, 3–4
unstageability of, 114–17
. *See also Richard II*; *Richard III*
Hobsbawm, Eric, 3, 31–33
Holbein, Hans, 122
Holderness, Graham, 109–10
Hortmann, Wilhelm, 120n32
Hugo, Victor, 7

I

immigrants. *See* integration of immigrants
indispensable unstageability
Histories and, 115–17
'Wars of the Roses' cycle, RSC, and, 116–17
Industrial Revolution, 141–42
In Parenthesis (Jones), 6, 95–104
integration of immigrants, tercentenary celebrations (1916) and, 78–79, 87
invented tradition, 3, 32–33
Irving, Henry, 62n13

J

Jackson, Barry, 4, 109, 112–13
Jackson, Philip Ward, 43, 61n4
Jardin Shakespeare (Bois de Boulogne), 7
Jones, David
Celtdom and, 94, 97
Henry V and, 6, 95–104
In Parenthesis, 6, 95–104
Malory and, 98, 100–101
national identity, Welsh, and, 94, 97, 100–104

World War I and, 95–97
As You Like It and, 98
Jonson, Ben, 16
Joughin, John, 110

K

Kahn, Coppélia, 78–79, 93, 100
Kean, Charles, 33–34, 36, 39n53, 39n56
Koch, Frederick, 82–83, 86–88

L

Laqueur, Thomas, 2
Leerssen, Joep, 2
libraries, women's clubs founding, 68–69
Lindbury Studio Theatre (Covent Garden), 4
'Little Gidding' (Eliot), 60, 62n23
local identities, tercentenary celebrations (1916) and, 83–88
London Olympics (2012), 9, 140
Brunel and, 141–44
Industrial Revolution and, 141–42
The Tempest and, 9, 141
Lukes, Steven, 30

M

Macbeth (Shakespeare), 31
MacKaye, Percy, 5, 79
community drama and, 86, 92n49
Maguire, Laurie, 43, 50
Malory, Thomas, 98, 100–101
masquerades
Great Shakespeare Jubilee (1769) and, 31
Royal Gala (1830) and, 32–36
masques
Caliban by the Yellow Sands (MacKaye), 5, 79, 86, 92n49
tercentenary celebrations (1916) and, 79–88
Massachusetts, tercentenary celebrations (1916) in, 80, 83–84
memorization, women's clubs and, 70
The Merry Wives of Windsor (Shakespeare), 31

Michelangelo, 122
A Midsummer Night's Dream (Shakespeare), 81
modernity
    of Elizabeth, age of, 122–23
    of Shakespeare, 123, 128, 138
Molière (Jean-Baptiste Poquelin), 8
monumental plays, *Henry VI* as, 107–17
Morley, George, 36, 39n72
Much Ado About Nothing (Shakespeare), 14
    forgetting in, 2
Murphy, Andrew, 110

N

narration in Sonnets, 1
Nashe, Thomas, 17–18, 108
national identity, American, tercentenary celebrations (1916) and, 82–83
national identity, British, 101, 137
    cycle performances and, 109–12, 115–16
    Henry V and, 93–94, 100
    Henry VI and, 112–13
    tercentenary celebrations (1916) and, 93–94
national identity, Welsh, 94, 97, 100–104
nationalism, Royal Gala of 1830 and, 32
Native Americans, tercentenary celebrations (1916) and, 78–79, 81, 87–89, 92nn59–60
Newstok, Scott, 14–15
North Dakota, tercentenary celebrations (1916) in, 81–83, 86–89, 92nn59–60

O

Othello (Shakespeare), 86

P

pageantry
    tercentenary celebrations (1916) and, 79–81
    . *See also* masques
Palmer, Leigh Anne, 77n49
patronage, First Folio monument and, 42
Paul (Saint), 56–57
Paul Fournier Shakespeare statue (Paris), 6–7
Paxton, Joseph, 131
Pericles (Shakespeare), 14
Periwinkle, Pauline, 82
plague, Elizabeth, age of, and, 134
private commemorations by women's clubs, 70
public commemorations by women's clubs, 66–69
public service by women's clubs, 66–69
Puttenham, George, 16

Q

Quayle, Anthony, 4, 109, 114, 116
Quoting Death (Newstok), 14

R

Racine, Jean, 8
Raleigh, Walter, 122
Rep. *See* Birmingham Repertory Theatre
Richard II (Shakespeare), 17
Richard III (Shakespeare), 17
Rigney, Ann, 2
rituals of commemoration
    Connerton on, 3, 30–32, 35, 74, 77nn56
    women's clubs and, 74–75
Robert Burns Centenary Festival (1859), 8
Rose Theatre (Kingston), 119n24
Rousseau, Jean-Jacques, 7–8
Rowlands, Michael, 68
Royal Festival Hall, Festival of Britain (1951) and, 136–37
Royal Gala (1830), 3, 28, 39n48
    dramatic procession in, 32–34
    masquerade ball in, 32–36
    nationalism and, 32
    plays performed during, 34, 36, 39n53
    Shakespeare as playwright transcended in, 36
    toasts in, 34–35
Royal Shakespeare Company (RSC), 108–9, 116–17, 118n5

S

Sardou, Victorien, 7
Schiller, Friedrich, 8
scholarships, women's clubs establishing, 68
scrapbooking, women's clubs and, 71–74, 77n49
September 11, 2001, 55
    Ground Zero, excavation of, and, 56
sermons, epitaphs in, 25n9
Shakespeare, the Playmaker (Koch), 81, 86–88
Shakespeare, William
    Antony and Cleopatra, 63n34
    As You Like It, 36, 98
    Comedy of Errors, 36
    Cymbeline, 25n9
    Hamlet, 1, 14, 36, 128–29
    Henry IV, 25n9
    Henry V, 2, 18–19, 22–24, 93–104
    Henry VI, 17, 20–22, 107–17, 119n24
    Histories, 1–4, 15, 108–17, 118n5, 118n8, 119n31
    Macbeth, 31, 67
    The Merchant of Venice, 67
    The Merry Wives of Windsor, 31
    A Midsummer Night's Dream, 81
    Much Ado About Nothing, 2, 14
    Othello, 86
    Pericles, 14
    Richard II, 17
    Richard III, 17
    Romeo and Juliet, 36, 67
    Sonnets, 1, 6, 14, 37
    The Tempest, 5, 81–83, 141
    Twelfth Night, 36, 72
    . *See also specific topics*
Shakespeare gardens, women's clubs and, 67
Shakespeare Memorial Theatre (SMT), 4, 109, 112–16
Sherman, Anita Gilman, 14
SMT. *See* Shakespeare Memorial Theatre
social memory, 77n54

La Songe d'une nuit d'été (Thomas), 4
Sonnet 55 (Shakespeare), 6
Sonnets (Shakespeare), 14
    narration in, 1
St Mary's church, ruins of, 46–48, 51–58, 63n36
Stubbs, William, 93
Summerson, John, 46

T

The Tempest (Shakespeare)
    London Olympics, 2012, and, 141
    tercentenary celebrations (1916) and, 81–83
tercentenary celebration (1864), 36, 38n16, 39n72
tercentenary celebrations (1916), 5–6
    African Americans and, 85–86, 91n45
    Caliban by the Yellow Sands in, 5, 79, 86
    class and, 85
    Drama League of America and, 83
    in Georgia, 80, 84–86
    integration of immigrants and, 78–79, 87
    local identities and, 83–88
    masques and, 79–88
    in Massachusetts, 80, 83–84
    national identity, American, and, 82–83
    national identity, British, and, 93–94
    Native Americans and, 78–79, 81, 87–89, 92nn59–60
    in North Dakota, 81–83, 86–89, 92nn59–60
    Othello and, 86
    pageantry and, 79–81
    The Tempest and, 81–83
Théâtre Impérial de Compiègne, 4
Thelen, David, 74
Thomas, Ambroise, 4
toasts, Royal Gala of 1830 and, 34–35
tombstones, 15
    First Folio monument (1896) as, 45

U

unstageability
    Histories and, 114–17
    indispensable, 115–17

V

Vauxhall Gardens, 8
Vichy government, France, 6–8
Villon, François, 8
Voltaire (François Marie Arouet), 8

W

Walker, Charles Clement, 43–45, 49, 53–54, 58–59, 62nn28–29, 63n34
Wallace, Jennifer, 55–56
Wardle, Irving, 117
war memorials
    churches, ruined, as, 46–48, 51–60, 63n45
    First Folio monument (1896) as, 45, 51–60
    Ground Zero, excavation of, as, 56
    World War I and, 51
    World War II and, 46–48, 51–60, 63n45
'Wars of the Roses' cycle, RSC, 108–9, 116–17, 118n5
Waugh, Evelyn, 58
Weever, John, 49–50
Wells, H. G., 9
William Shakespeare locomotive, 137–38
Wilson, J. Dover, 115
Winter, Jay, 2

women's clubs, 5, 65
    collective memory and, 74–75
    cooking and, 71–72
    domestic commemorations by, 71–75
    First Folio purchased by, 69
    libraries founded by, 68–69
    memorization and, 70
    private commemorations by, 70
    public commemorations by, 66–69
    rituals of commemoration and, 74–75
    scholarships established by, 68
    scrapbooking by, 71–74, 77n49
    Shakespeare gardens and, 67
    World War I and, 66
    World War II and, 66
World War I, 5–6
    Jones and, 95–97
    war memorials and, 51
    women's clubs and, 66
World War II, 135–36
    war memorials and, 46–48, 51–60, 63n45
    women's clubs and, 66
Wren, Christopher, 46
Wright, Louis B., 70

Y

Y Gododdin, 101
Young, William A., 48, 63n36

Z

Zola, Émile, 8

www.ingramcontent.com/pod-product-compliance
Lightning Source LLC
Chambersburg PA
CBHW070043120526
44589CB00035B/2292